The Titanic

written by
Joe Dunn
illustrated by
Ben Dunn

visit us at
www.abdopublishing.com

Published by Magic Wagon, a division of the ABDO Publishing Group, 8000 West 78th Street, Edina, Minnesota 55439. Copyright © 2008 by Abdo Consulting Group, Inc. International copyrights reserved in all countries.

Printed in the United States.

Written by Joe Dunn
Illustrated by Ben Dunn
Colored by Robby Bevard
Lettered by Joe Dunn
Cover art by Ben Dunn and GURU-eFX
Edited by Stephanie Hedlund
Interior layout and design by Antarctic Press
Cover art by Ben Dunn
Cover design by Neil Klinepier

Library of Congress Cataloging-in-Publication Data

Dunn, Joeming W.
     The Titanic / written by Joe Dunn ; illustrated by Ben Dunn.
     p. cm. -- (Graphic history)
     Includes index.
     ISBN 978-1-60270-079-6
     1. Titanic (Steamship)--Juvenile literature. 2. Shipwrecks--North Atlantic Ocean--Juvenile literature. I. Dunn, Ben, ill. II. Title.
   G530.T6D86 2008
   910.9163'4--dc22
                                                                    2007012066

TABLE of CONTENTS

Timeline...4

Chapter 1
   Building of a Mighty Ship...............................5

Chapter 2
   Queen of the Oceans....................................7

Chapter 3
   The Maiden Voyage....................................10

Chapter 4
   Iceberg Dead Ahead!..................................14

Chapter 5
   Women and Children First!...........................18

Chapter 6
   The Sinking of the Unsinkable.......................24

Chapter 7
   Rescued at Last.......................................27

Titanic Facts...29

Route of the *Titanic*...30

Glossary..31

Web Sites..31

Index..32

Timeline

1909 - Construction of the *Titanic* began in Belfast, Ireland.

1911 - The hull of *Titanic* was successfully launched.

January 1912 - Sixteen wooden and four collapsible lifeboats were fitted aboard the *Titanic*.

April 10, 1912, 9:30-11:30 AM - Passengers arrived in Southampton and boarded ship.

April 10, 1912, 12:00 PM - The *Titanic* began its maiden voyage.

April 12-13, 1912 - The *Titanic* sailed through calm waters.

April 14, 11:40 PM - The lookouts spotted an iceberg. The iceberg struck the *Titanic* on the starboard (right) side of her bow.

April 14, 11:50 PM - Water poured in and rose 14 feet in the front part of the ship.

April 15, 12:00 AM - The captain gave the order to call for help.

April 15, 12:05 AM - Orders were given to uncover the lifeboats and to get passengers and crew ready on deck.

April 15, 12:25 AM - Lifeboats were loaded with women and children first. The *Carpathia*, about 58 miles away, picked up the distress call.

April 15, 12:45 AM - The first lifeboat was safely lowered away. It could carry 65 people, but only had 28. The first distress rocket was fired.

April 15, 2:05 AM - The last lifeboat departed, leaving 1,500 people on the ship.

April 15, 2:20 AM - The *Titanic*'s broken-off stern settled back into the water. Slowly it filled with water and again tilted its end high into the air before sinking into the sea. People in the water slowly froze to death.

April 15, 4:10 AM - The first lifeboat was picked up by the *Carpathia*.

April 15, 8:50 AM - The *Carpathia* left for New York. She carried 705 survivors.

April 19-May 25, 1912 - Several ships were sent to the disaster site to recover bodies. A total of 328 bodies were found floating in the area.

Chapter 1 Building of a Mighty Ship

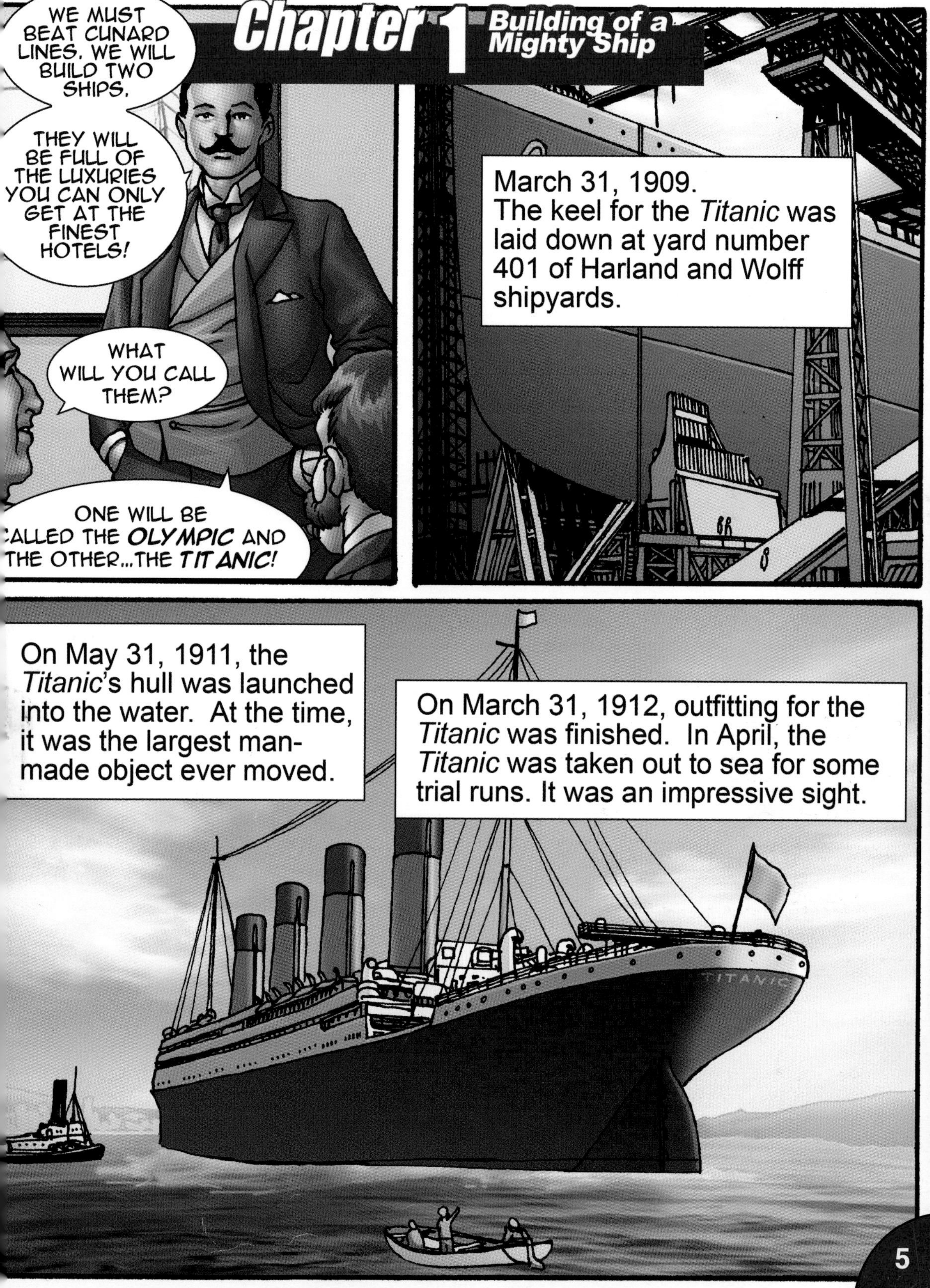

WE MUST BEAT CUNARD LINES. WE WILL BUILD TWO SHIPS.
THEY WILL BE FULL OF THE LUXURIES YOU CAN ONLY GET AT THE FINEST HOTELS!
WHAT WILL YOU CALL THEM?
ONE WILL BE ALLED THE *OLYMPIC* AND THE OTHER...THE *TITANIC*!
March 31, 1909. The keel for the *Titanic* was laid down at yard number 401 of Harland and Wolff shipyards.
On May 31, 1911, the *Titanic*'s hull was launched into the water. At the time, it was the largest man-made object ever moved.
On March 31, 1912, outfitting for the *Titanic* was finished. In April, the *Titanic* was taken out to sea for some trial runs. It was an impressive sight.
TITANIC

It was the largest ship ever made at the time. And it was advertised to be unsinkable.

Thomas Andrews designed the *Titanic*. He oversaw the ship's outfitting.

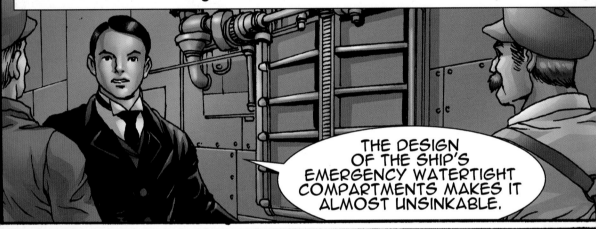

THE DESIGN OF THE SHIP'S EMERGENCY WATERTIGHT COMPARTMENTS MAKES IT ALMOST UNSINKABLE.

A SHIP THAT SIZE! IS IT SAFE?

THEY SAY IT IS UNSINKABLE.

HARPER'S WEEKLY
JOURNAL OF CIVILIZATION

UNSINKABLE SHIP "TITAN

THE TITANIC COMPARED WITH THE HOUSES

940 FEET

Chapter 2 Queen of the Oceans

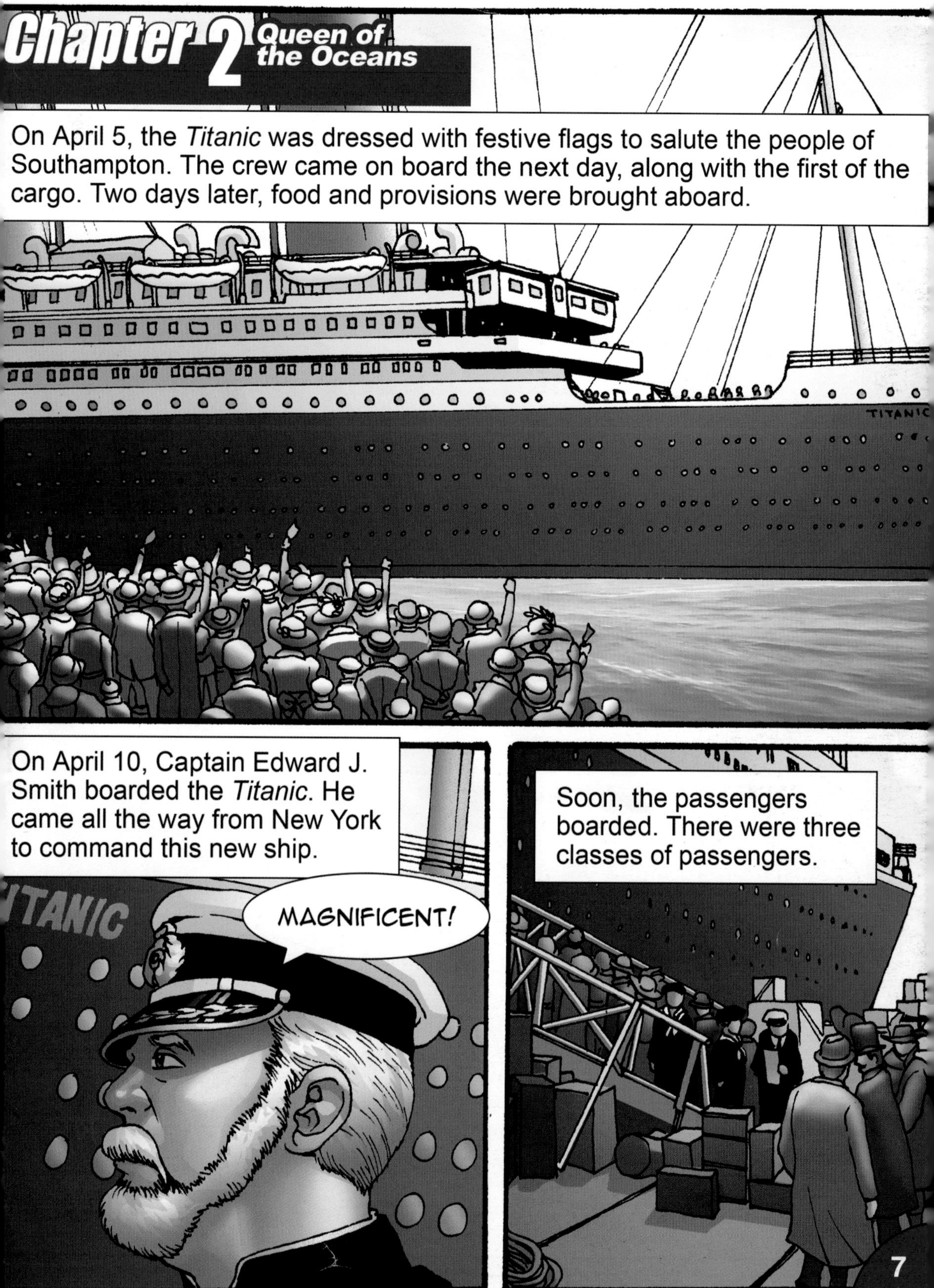
On April 5, the *Titanic* was dressed with festive flags to salute the people of Southampton. The crew came on board the next day, along with the first of the cargo. Two days later, food and provisions were brought aboard.
TITANIC
On April 10, Captain Edward J. Smith boarded the *Titanic*. He came all the way from New York to command this new ship.
TANIC
MAGNIFICENT!
Soon, the passengers boarded. There were three classes of passengers.

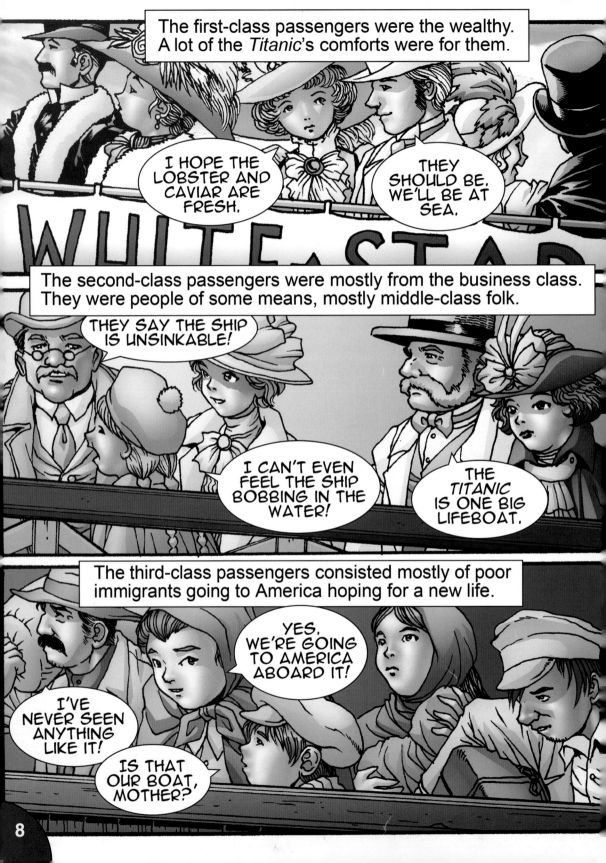

The first-class passengers were the wealthy. A lot of the *Titanic*'s comforts were for them.

I HOPE THE LOBSTER AND CAVIAR ARE FRESH.

THEY SHOULD BE, WE'LL BE AT SEA.

The second-class passengers were mostly from the business class. They were people of some means, mostly middle-class folk.

THEY SAY THE SHIP IS UNSINKABLE!

I CAN'T EVEN FEEL THE SHIP BOBBING IN THE WATER!

THE *TITANIC* IS ONE BIG LIFEBOAT.

The third-class passengers consisted mostly of poor immigrants going to America hoping for a new life.

YES, WE'RE GOING TO AMERICA ABOARD IT!

I'VE NEVER SEEN ANYTHING LIKE IT!

IS THAT OUR BOAT, MOTHER?

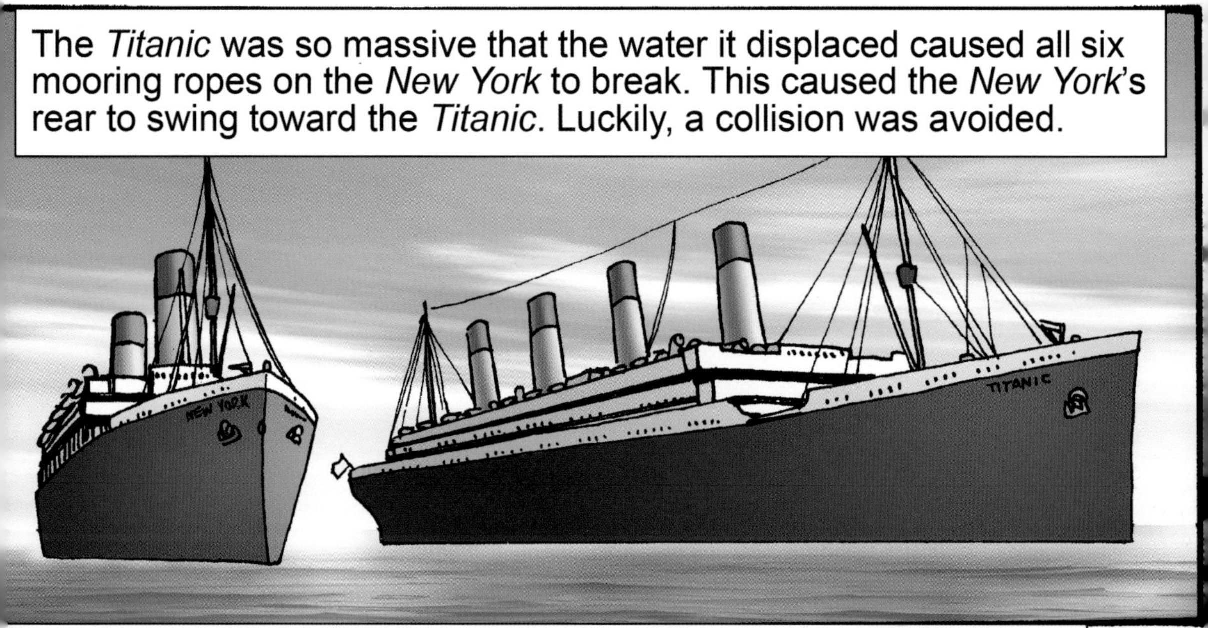
The *Titanic* was so massive that the water it displaced caused all six mooring ropes on the *New York* to break. This caused the *New York*'s rear to swing toward the *Titanic*. Luckily, a collision was avoided.
NEW YORK
TITANIC

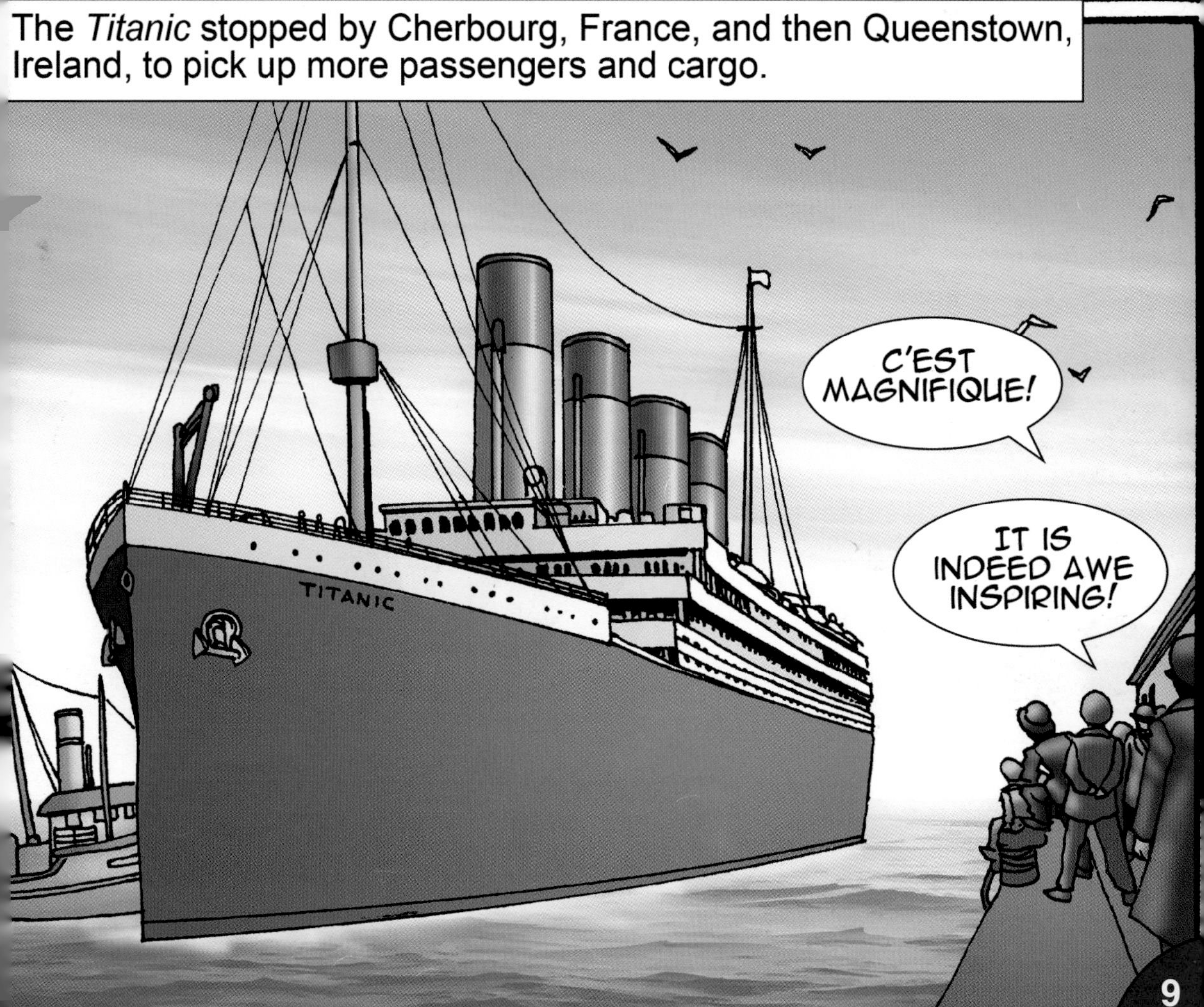
The *Titanic* stopped by Cherbourg, France, and then Queenstown, Ireland, to pick up more passengers and cargo.
C'EST MAGNIFIQUE!
IT IS INDEED AWE INSPIRING!
TITANIC

Chapter 3 The Maiden Voyage

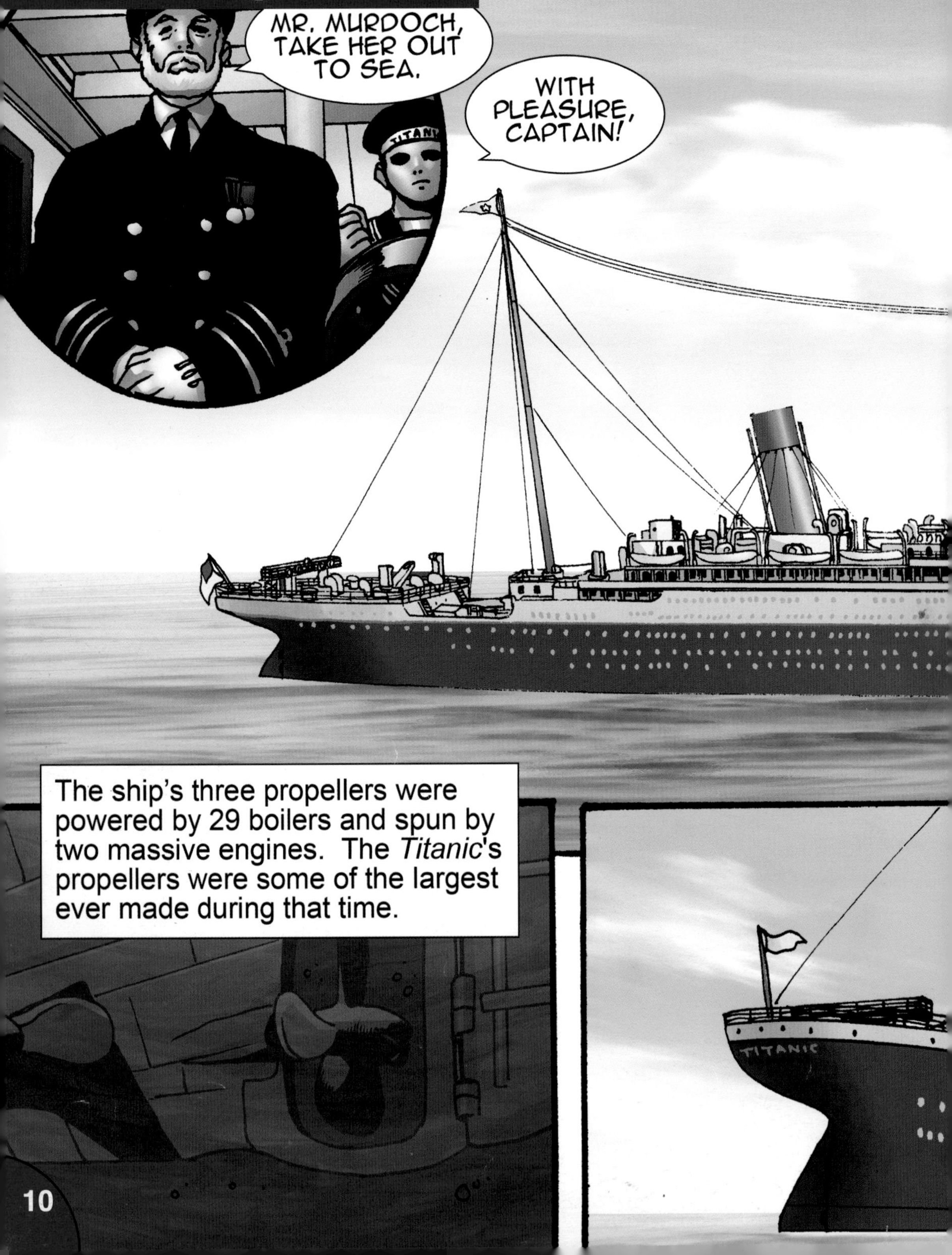
MR. MURDOCH, TAKE HER OUT TO SEA.
WITH PLEASURE, CAPTAIN!
The ship's three propellers were powered by 29 boilers and spun by two massive engines. The *Titanic*'s propellers were some of the largest ever made during that time.
TITANIC

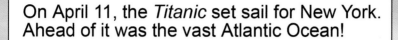

On April 11, the *Titanic* set sail for New York. Ahead of it was the vast Atlantic Ocean!

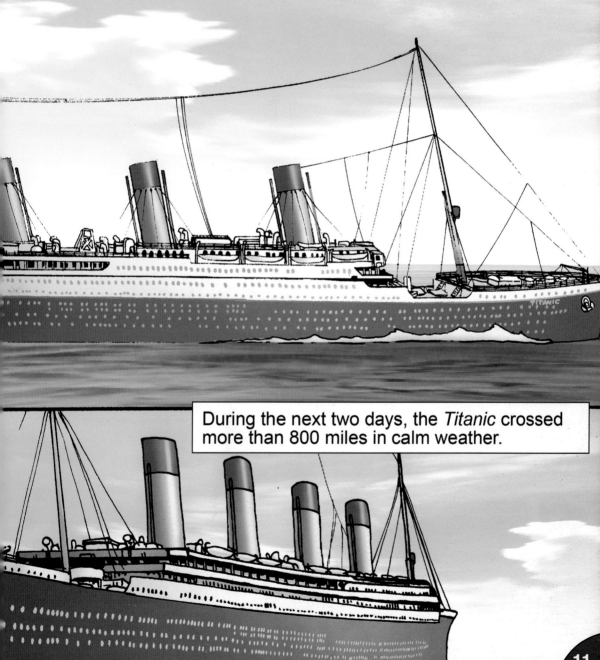

During the next two days, the *Titanic* crossed more than 800 miles in calm weather.

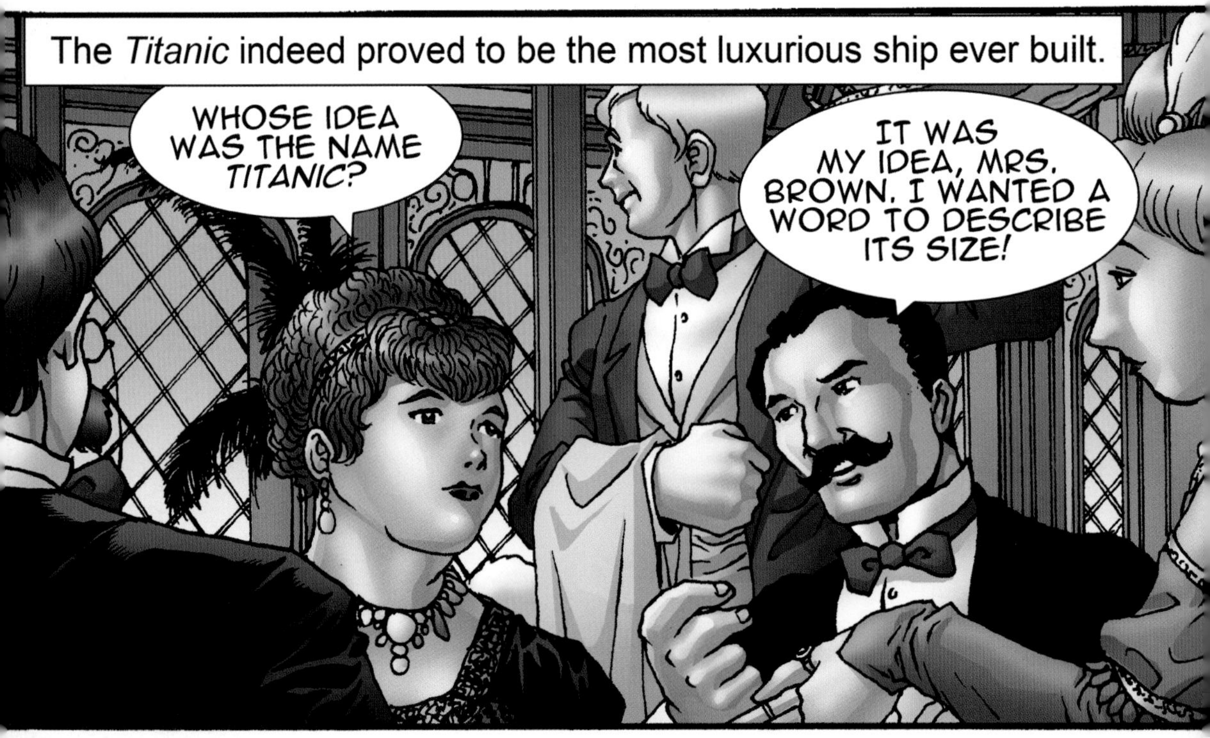
The *Titanic* indeed proved to be the most luxurious ship ever built.
WHOSE IDEA WAS THE NAME *TITANIC*?
IT WAS MY IDEA, MRS. BROWN. I WANTED A WORD TO DESCRIBE ITS SIZE!

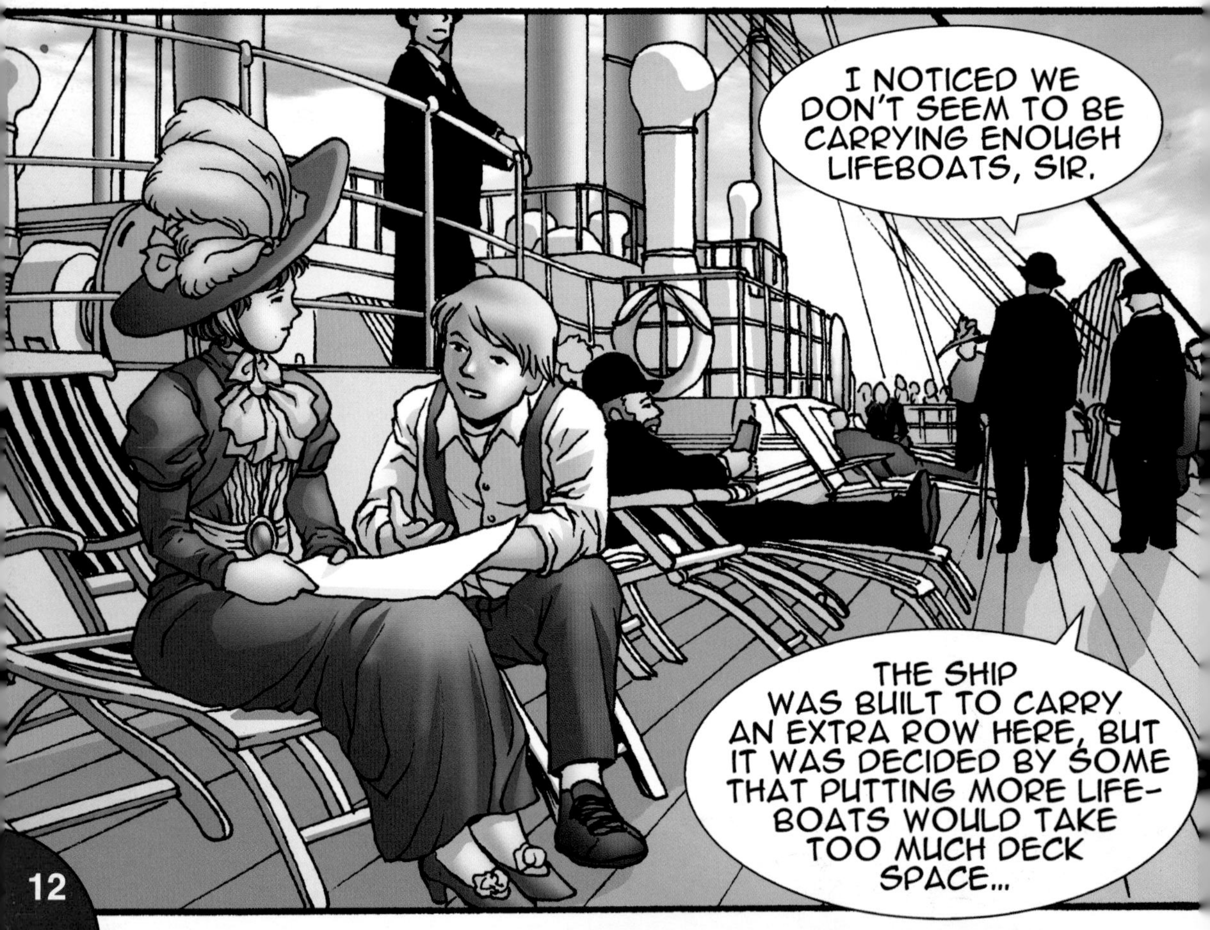
I NOTICED WE DON'T SEEM TO BE CARRYING ENOUGH LIFEBOATS, SIR.
THE SHIP WAS BUILT TO CARRY AN EXTRA ROW HERE, BUT IT WAS DECIDED BY SOME THAT PUTTING MORE LIFE-BOATS WOULD TAKE TOO MUCH DECK SPACE...

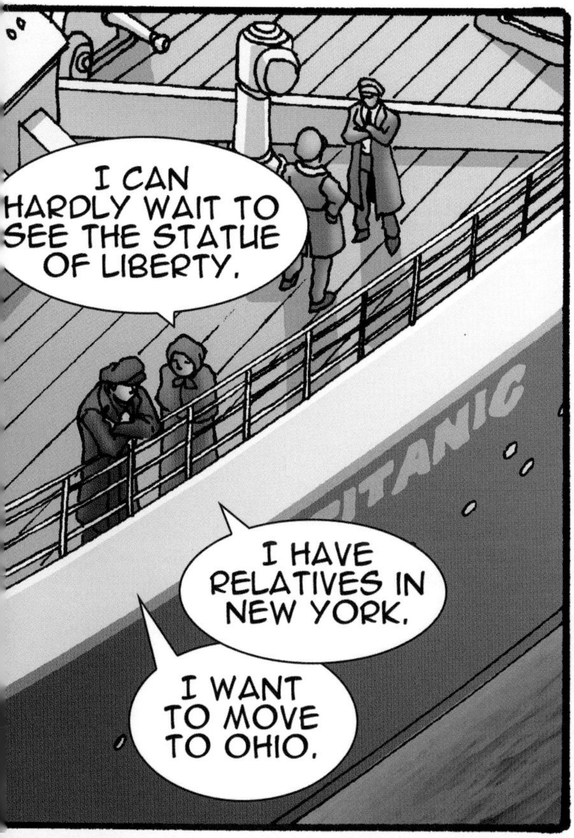
I CAN HARDLY WAIT TO SEE THE STATUE OF LIBERTY.
I HAVE RELATIVES IN NEW YORK.
I WANT TO MOVE TO OHIO.

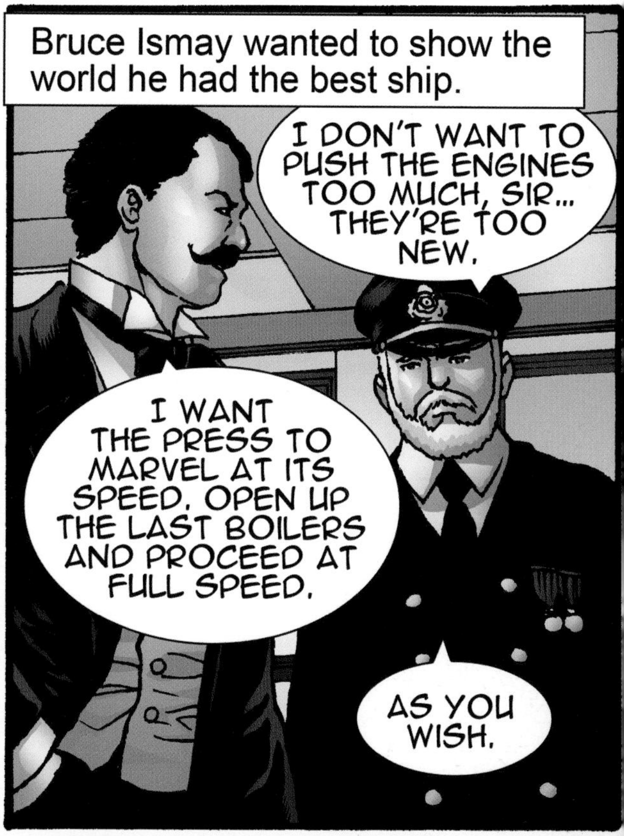
Bruce Ismay wanted to show the world he had the best ship.
I WANT THE PRESS TO MARVEL AT ITS SPEED. OPEN UP THE LAST BOILERS AND PROCEED AT FULL SPEED.
I DON'T WANT TO PUSH THE ENGINES TOO MUCH, SIR... THEY'RE TOO NEW.
AS YOU WISH.

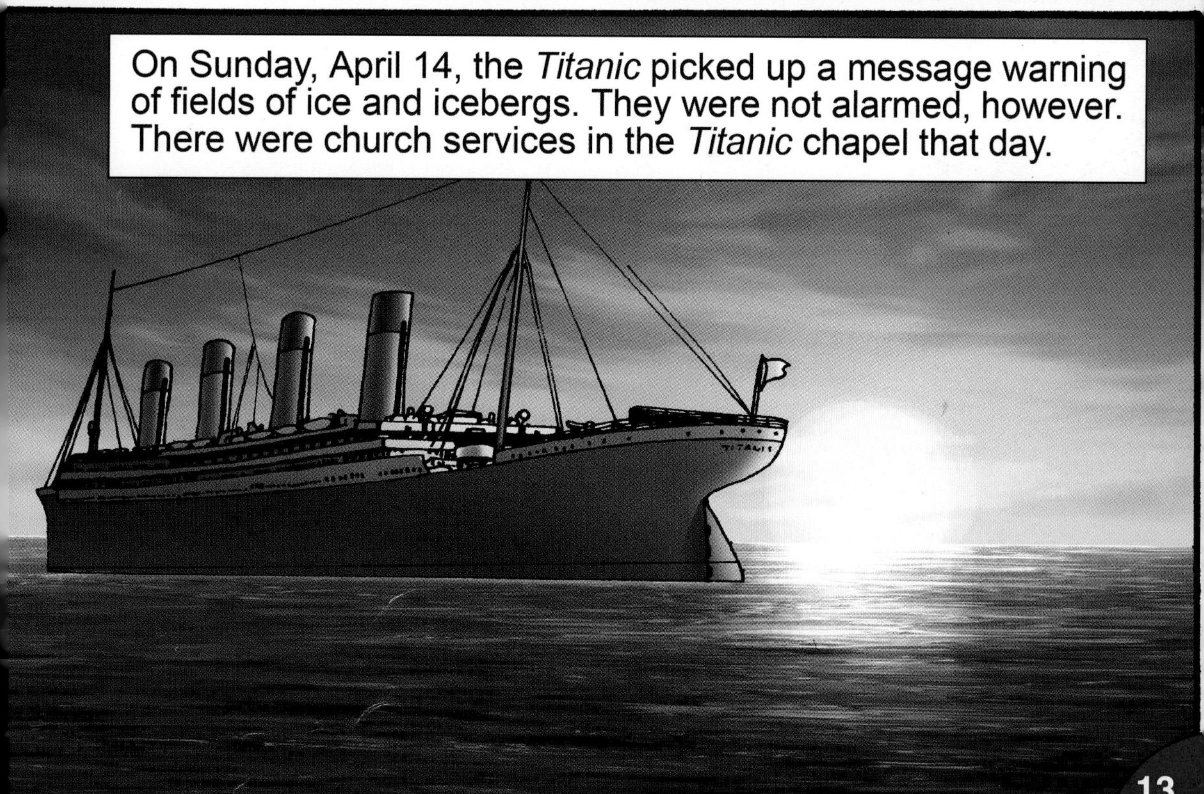
On Sunday, April 14, the *Titanic* picked up a message warning of fields of ice and icebergs. They were not alarmed, however. There were church services in the *Titanic* chapel that day.

Chapter 4 Iceberg Dead Ahead!

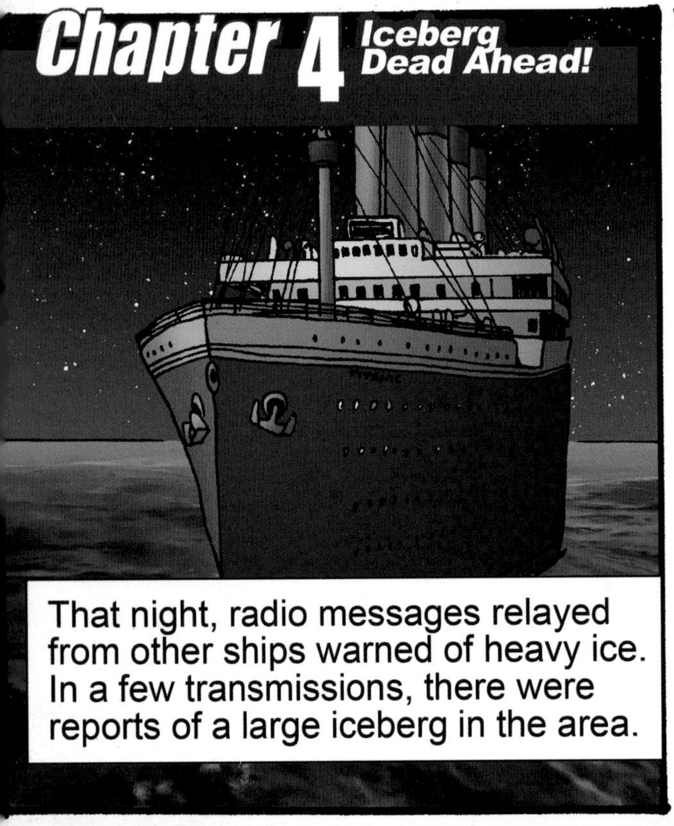
That night, radio messages relayed from other ships warned of heavy ice. In a few transmissions, there were reports of a large iceberg in the area.

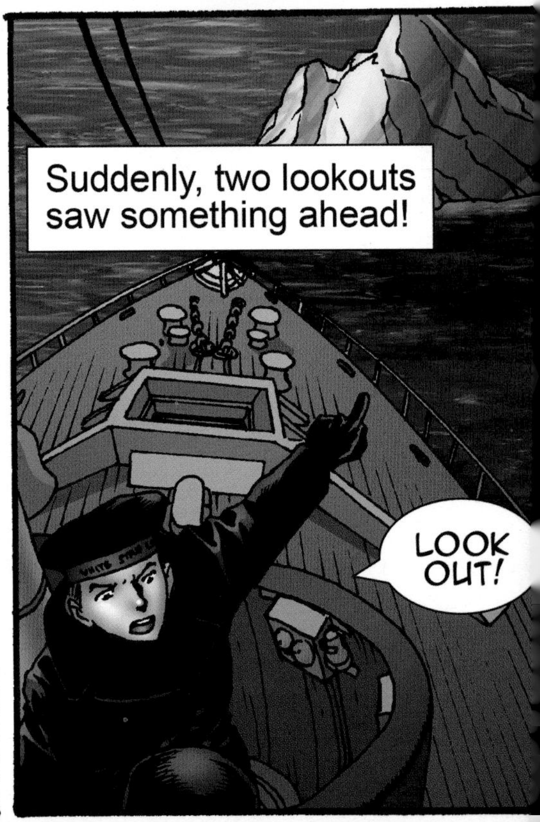
Suddenly, two lookouts saw something ahead!
LOOK OUT!

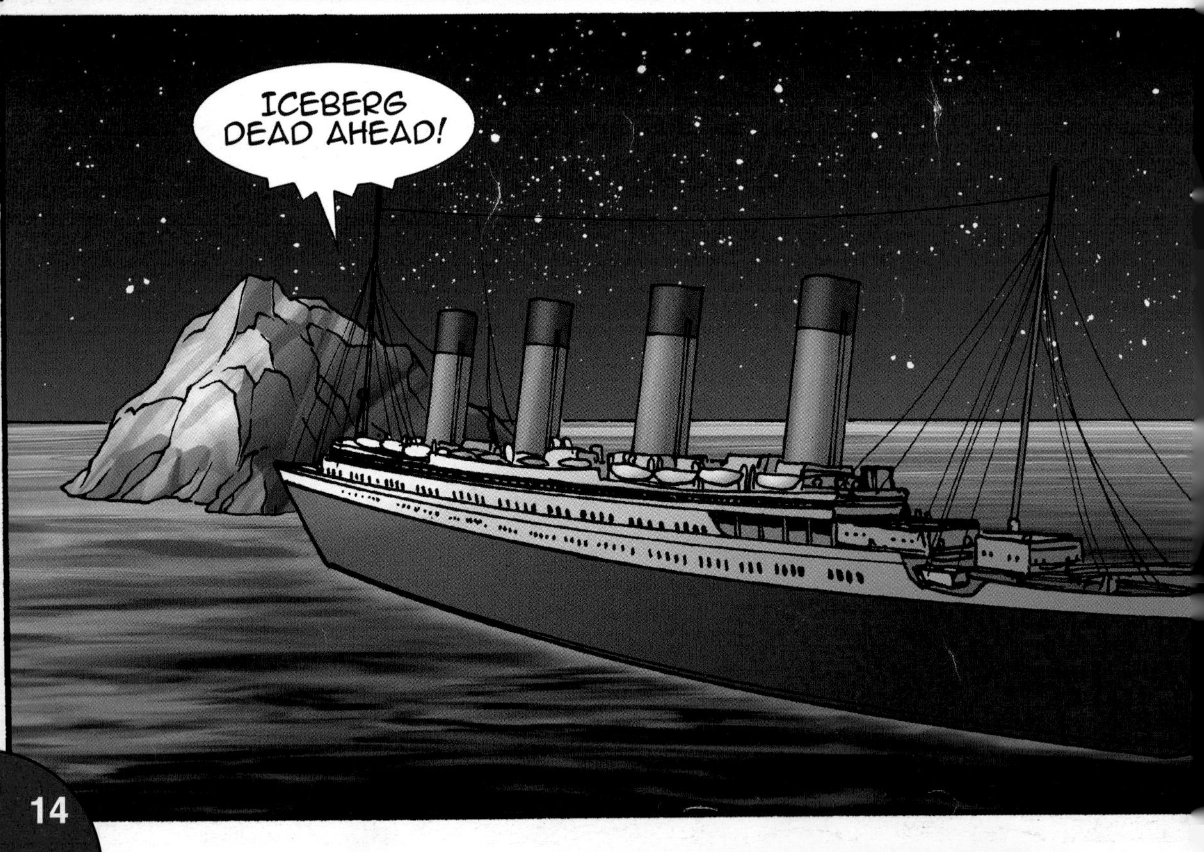
ICEBERG DEAD AHEAD!

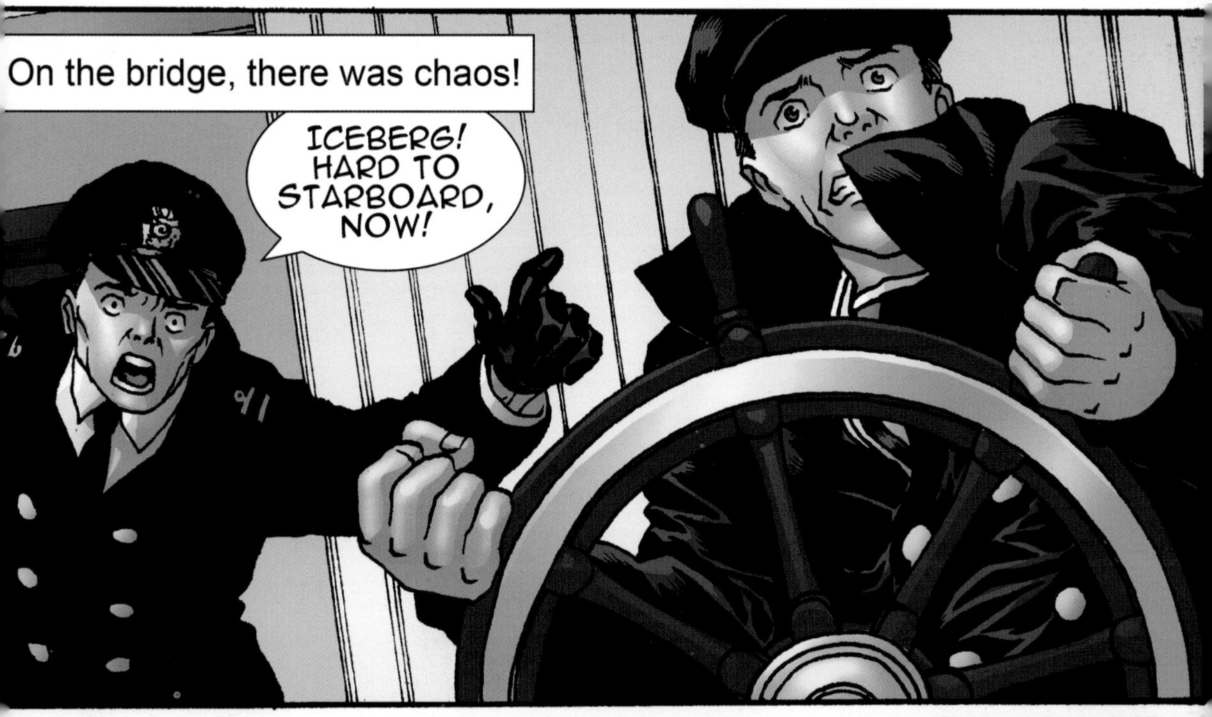
On the bridge, there was chaos!
ICEBERG! HARD TO STARBOARD, NOW!

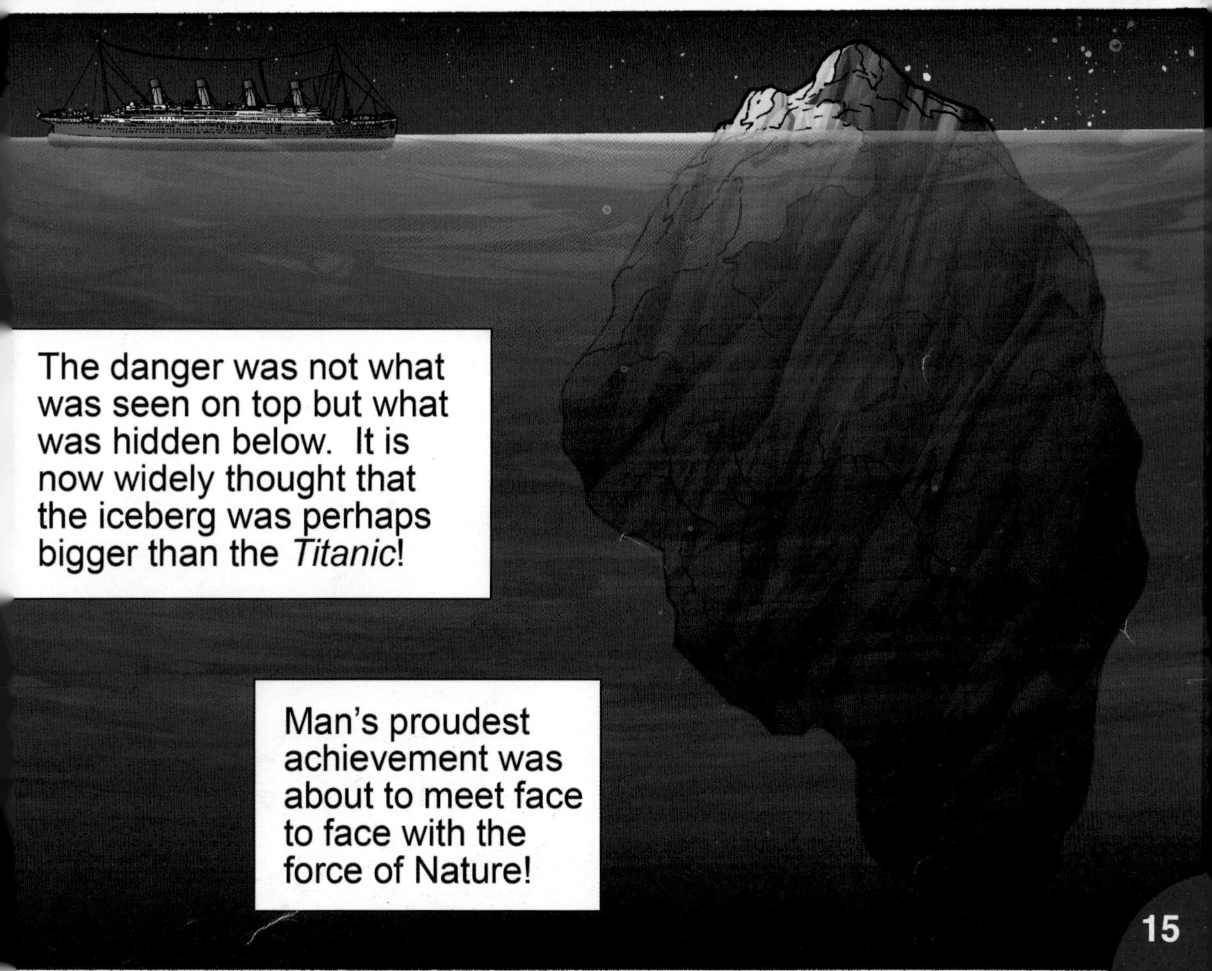
The danger was not what was seen on top but what was hidden below. It is now widely thought that the iceberg was perhaps bigger than the *Titanic*!
Man's proudest achievement was about to meet face to face with the force of Nature!

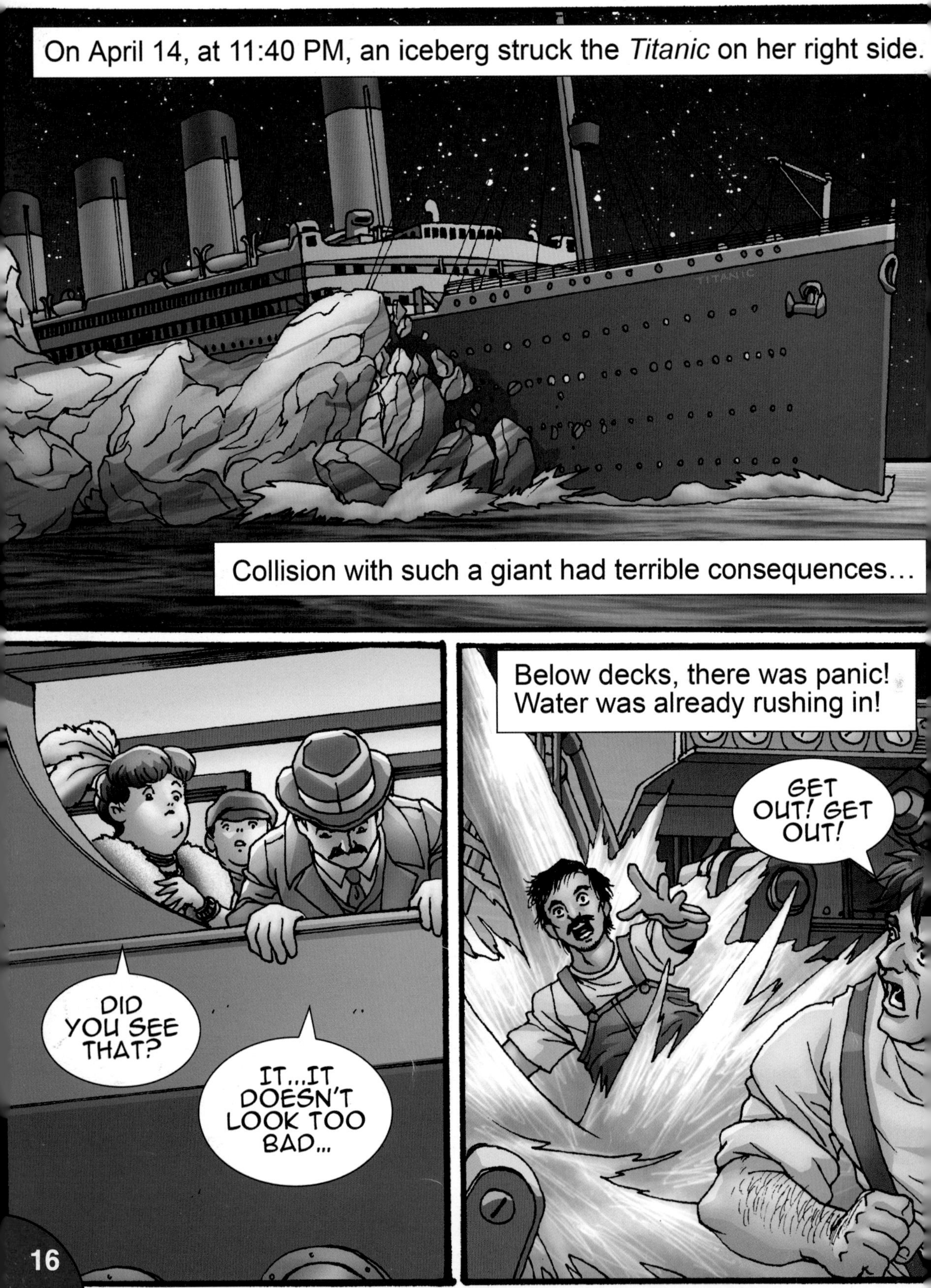
On April 14, at 11:40 PM, an iceberg struck the *Titanic* on her right side.
Collision with such a giant had terrible consequences…
DID YOU SEE THAT?
IT...IT DOESN'T LOOK TOO BAD...
Below decks, there was panic! Water was already rushing in!
GET OUT! GET OUT!

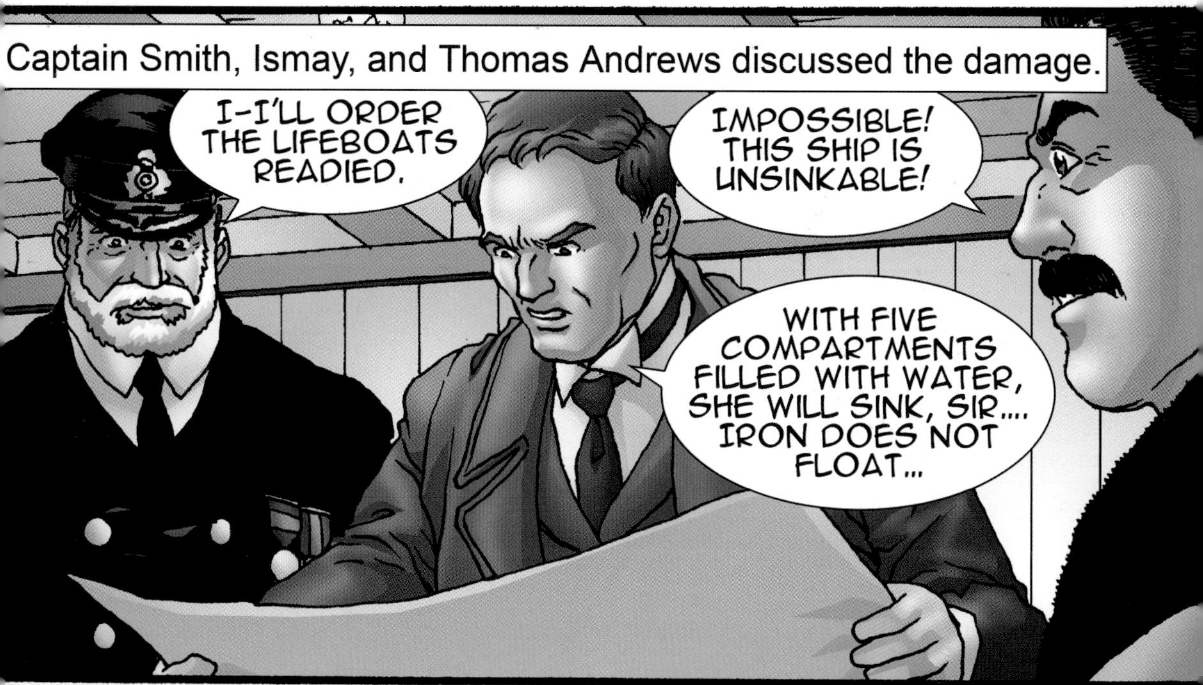
Captain Smith, Ismay, and Thomas Andrews discussed the damage.
I-I'LL ORDER THE LIFEBOATS READIED.
IMPOSSIBLE! THIS SHIP IS UNSINKABLE!
WITH FIVE COMPARTMENTS FILLED WITH WATER, SHE WILL SINK, SIR.... IRON DOES NOT FLOAT...

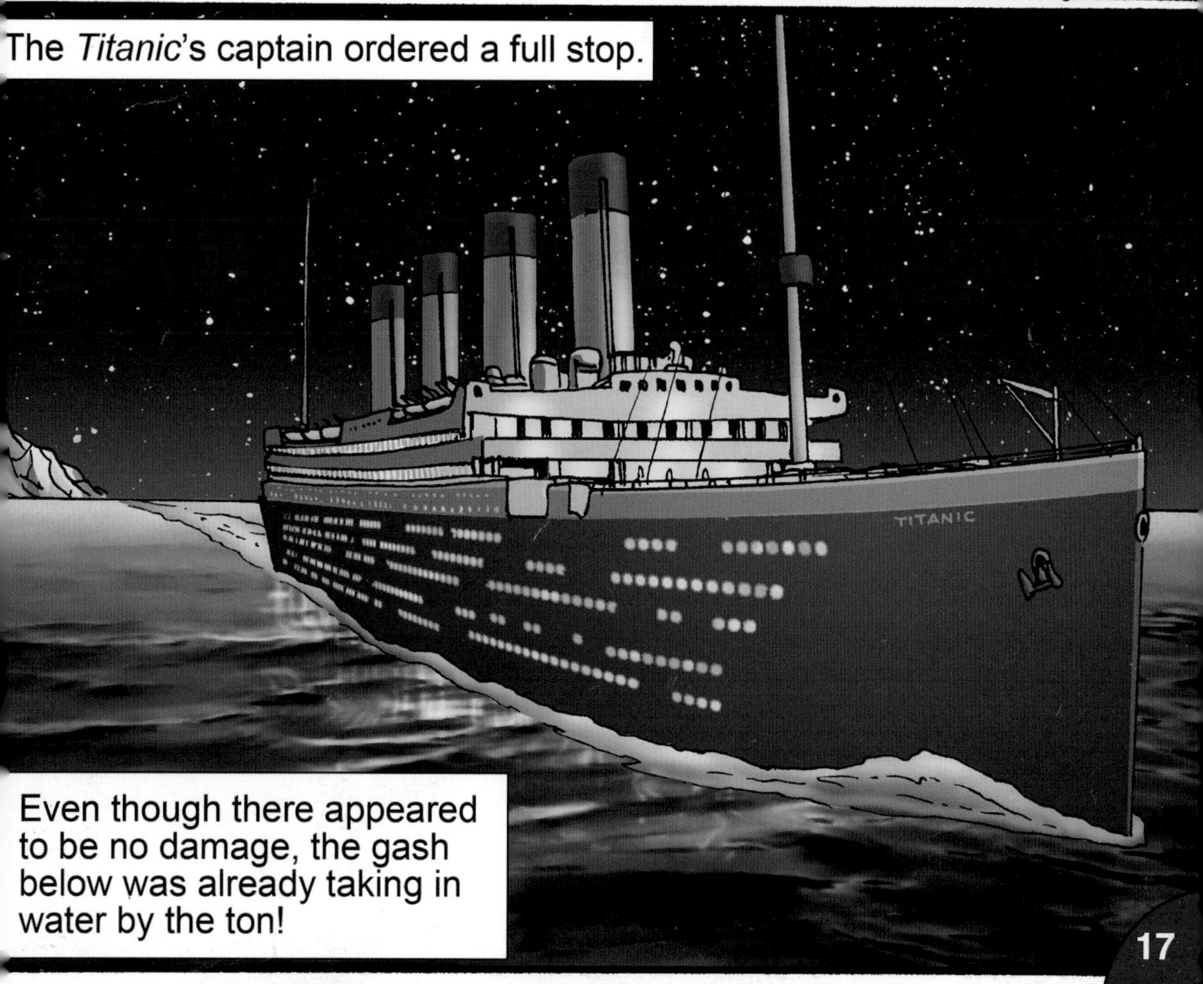
The *Titanic*'s captain ordered a full stop.
TITANIC
Even though there appeared to be no damage, the gash below was already taking in water by the ton!

Chapter 5 Women and Children First!

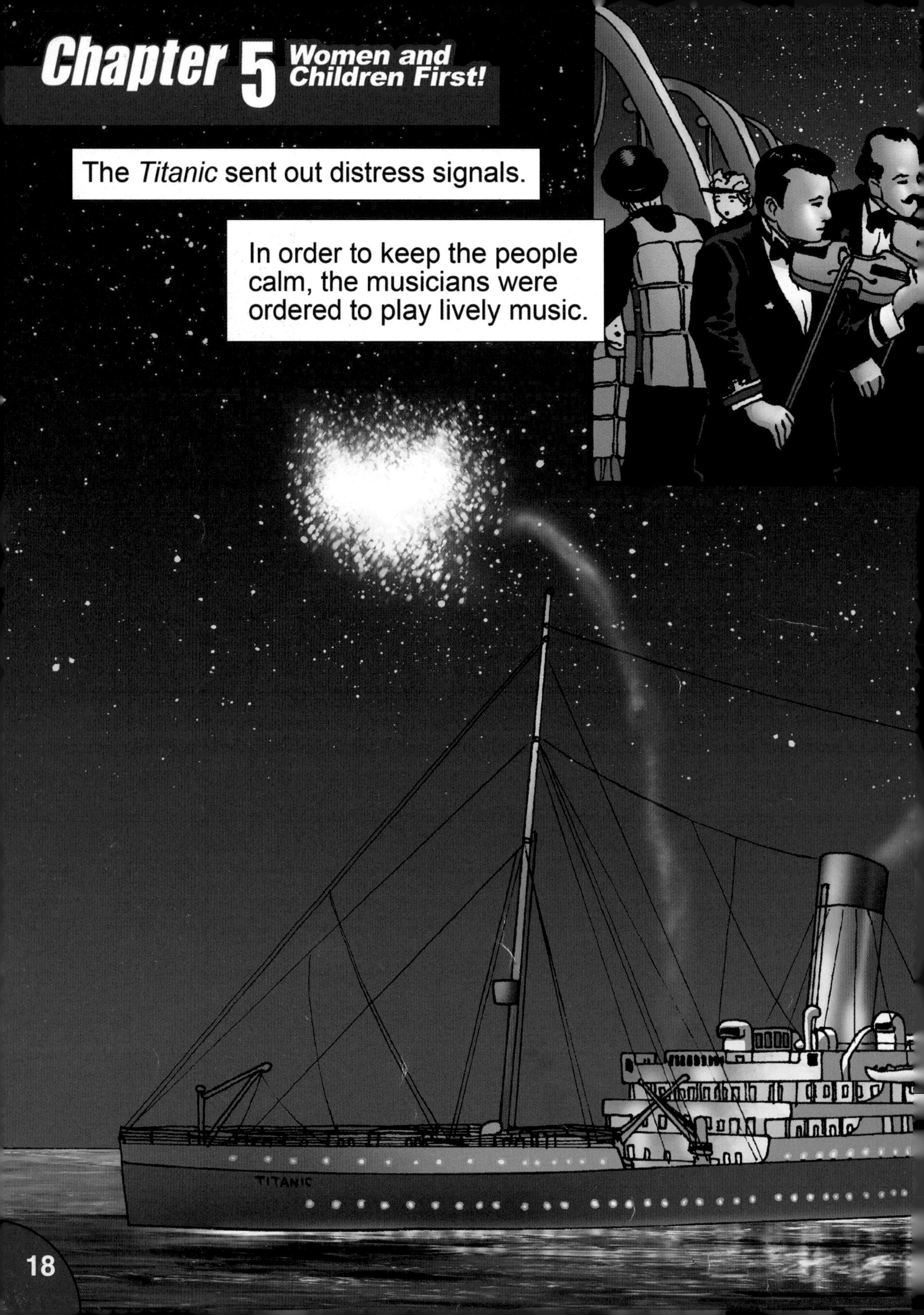
The *Titanic* sent out distress signals.
In order to keep the people calm, the musicians were ordered to play lively music.
TITANIC

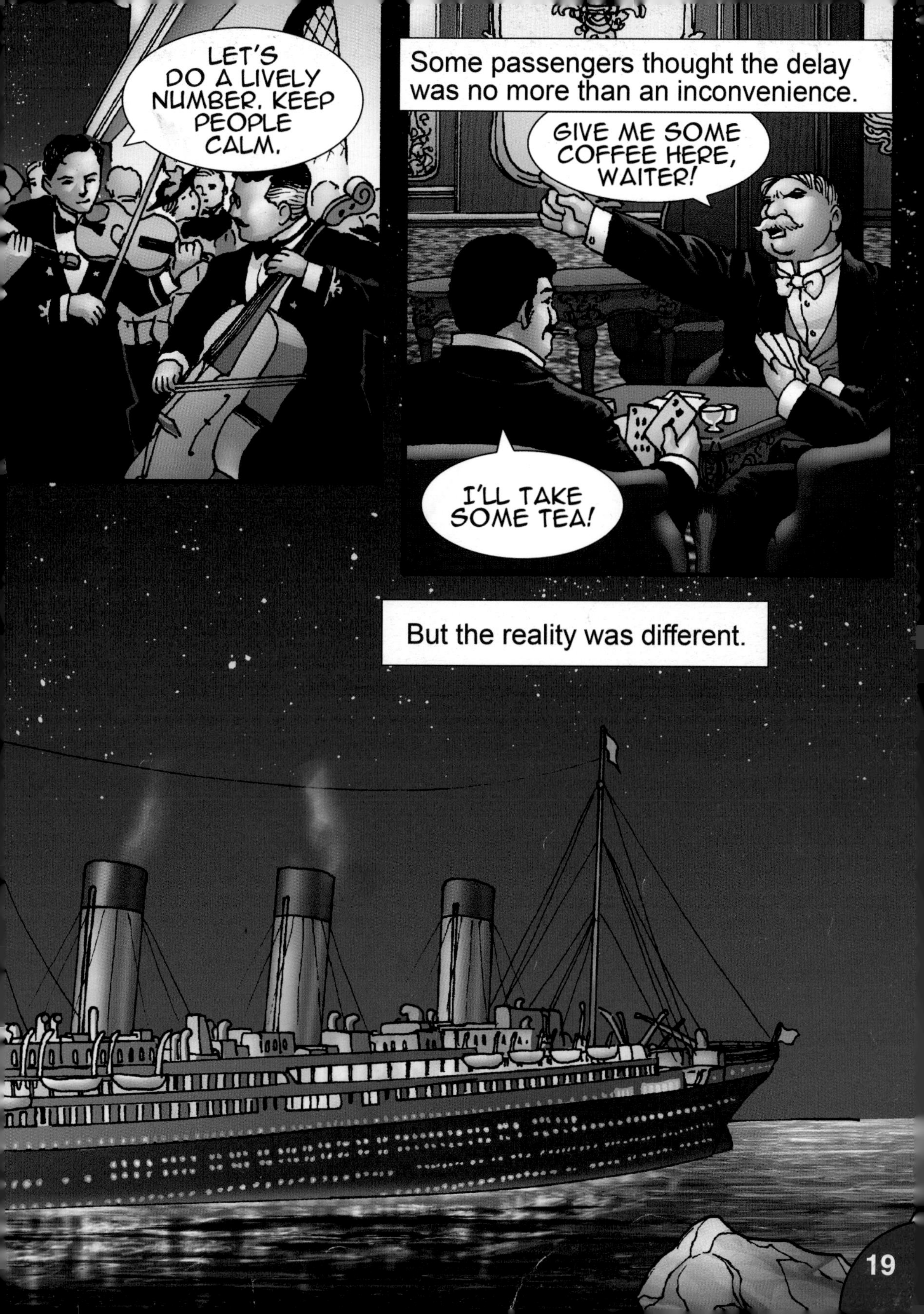

LET'S DO A LIVELY NUMBER. KEEP PEOPLE CALM.
Some passengers thought the delay was no more than an inconvenience.
GIVE ME SOME COFFEE HERE, WAITER!
I'LL TAKE SOME TEA!
But the reality was different.

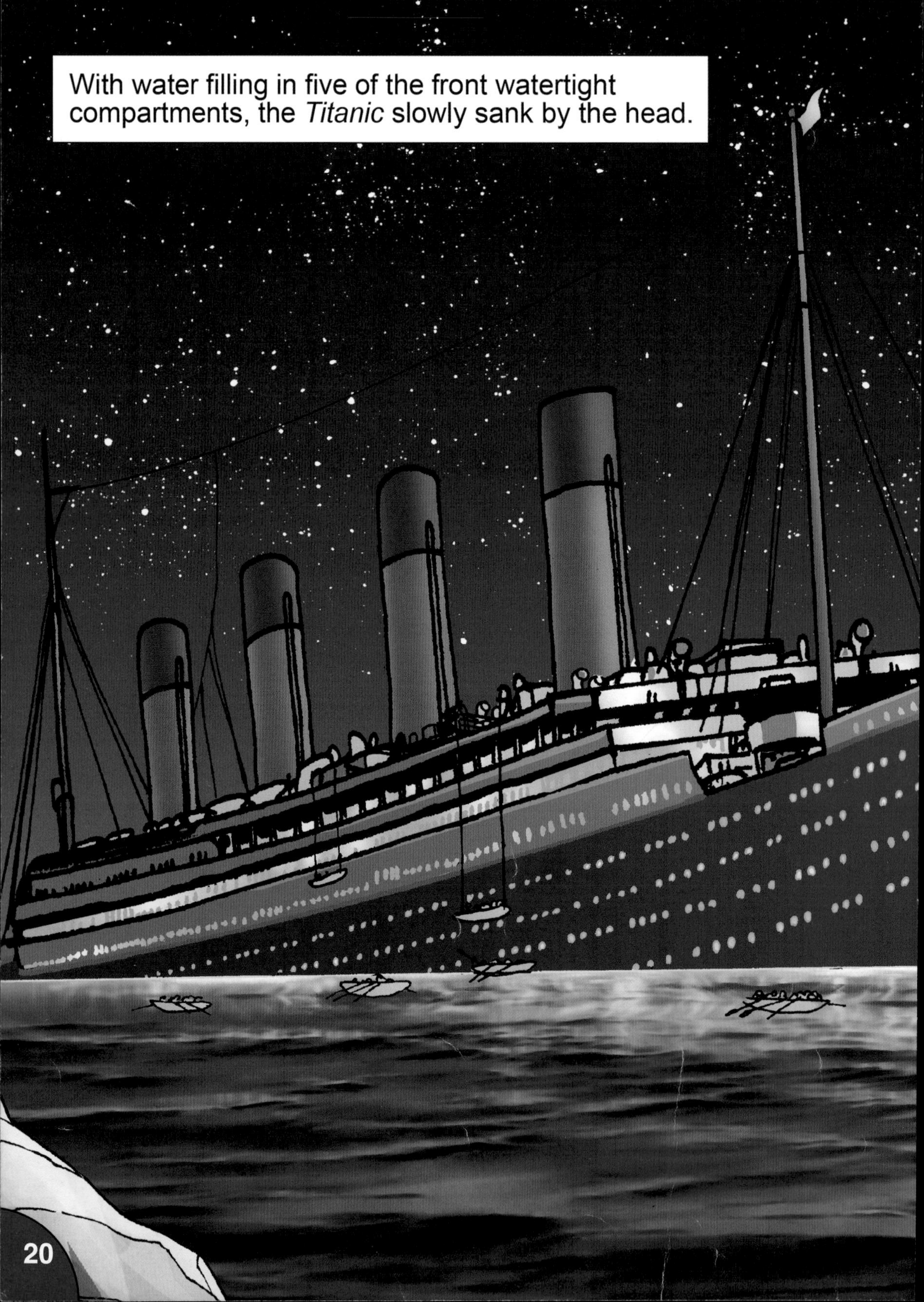
With water filling in five of the front watertight compartments, the Titanic slowly sank by the head.

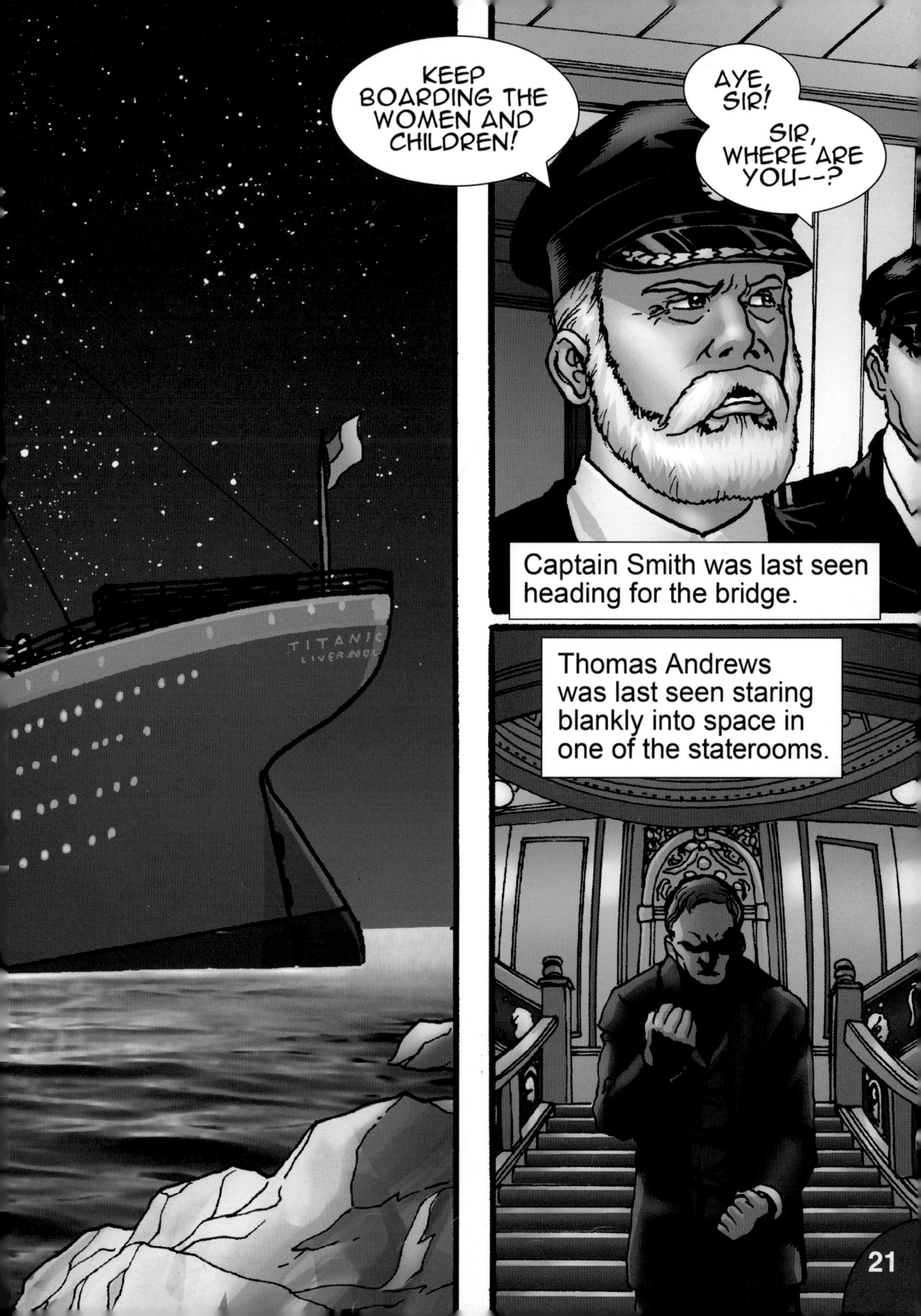
KEEP BOARDING THE WOMEN AND CHILDREN!
AYE, SIR!
SIR, WHERE ARE YOU--?
Captain Smith was last seen heading for the bridge.
Thomas Andrews was last seen staring blankly into space in one of the staterooms.

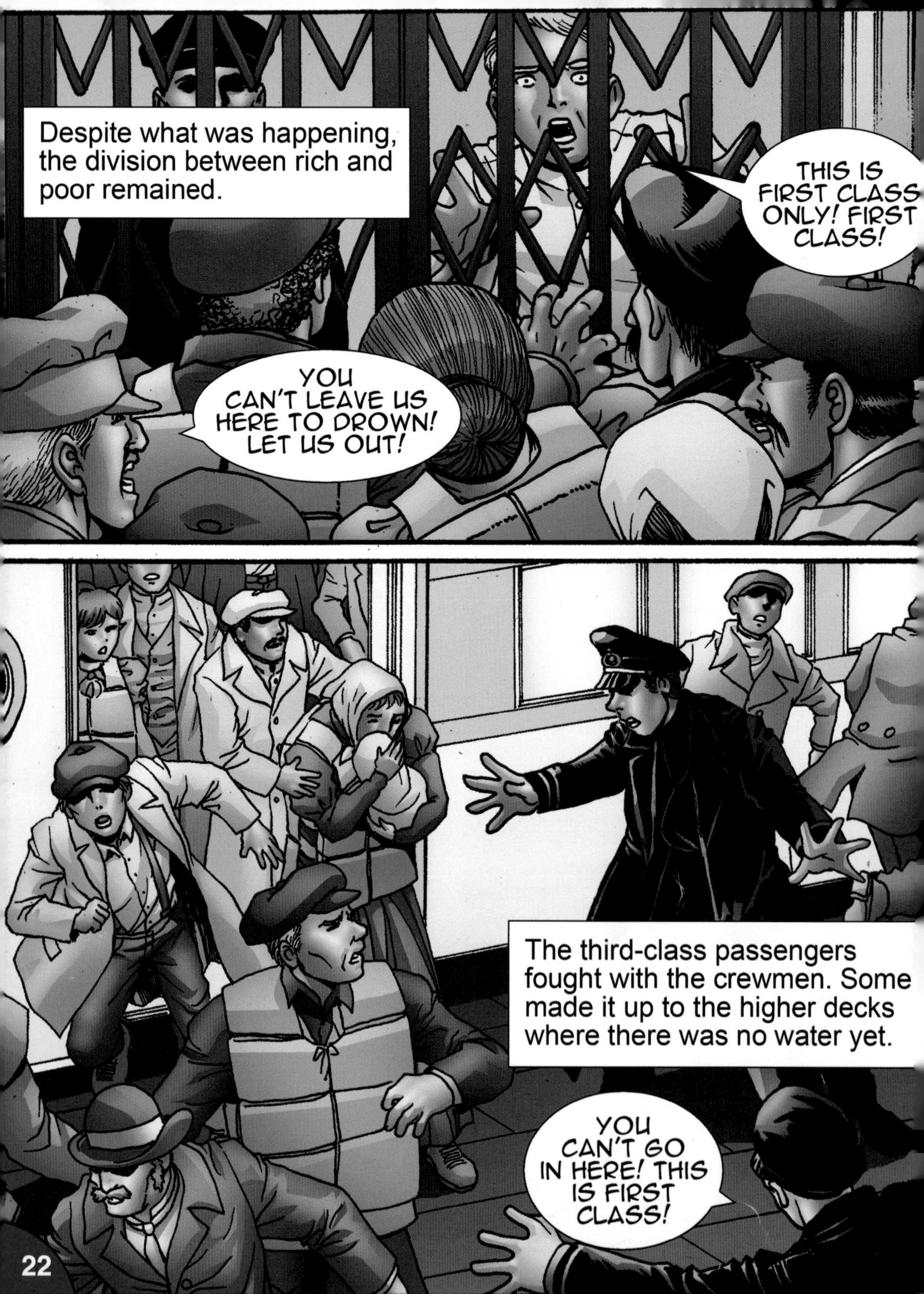
Despite what was happening, the division between rich and poor remained.
THIS IS FIRST CLASS ONLY! FIRST CLASS!
YOU CAN'T LEAVE US HERE TO DROWN! LET US OUT!
The third-class passengers fought with the crewmen. Some made it up to the higher decks where there was no water yet.
YOU CAN'T GO IN HERE! THIS IS FIRST CLASS!

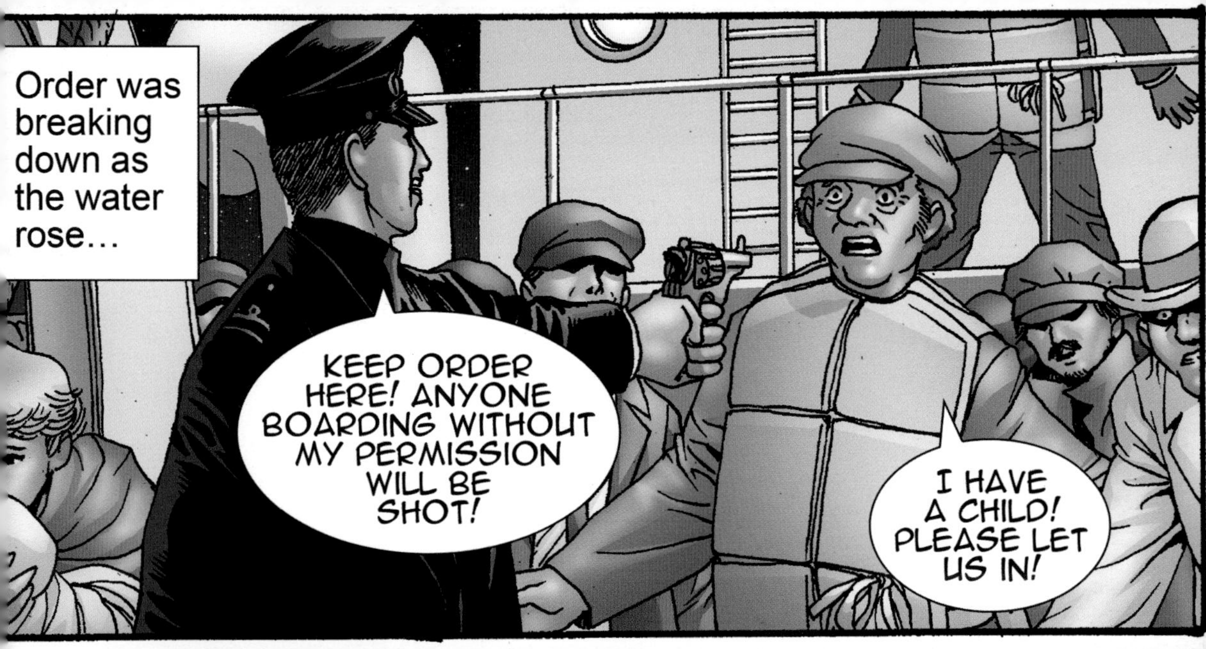
Order was breaking down as the water rose...
KEEP ORDER HERE! ANYONE BOARDING WITHOUT MY PERMISSION WILL BE SHOT!
I HAVE A CHILD! PLEASE LET US IN!

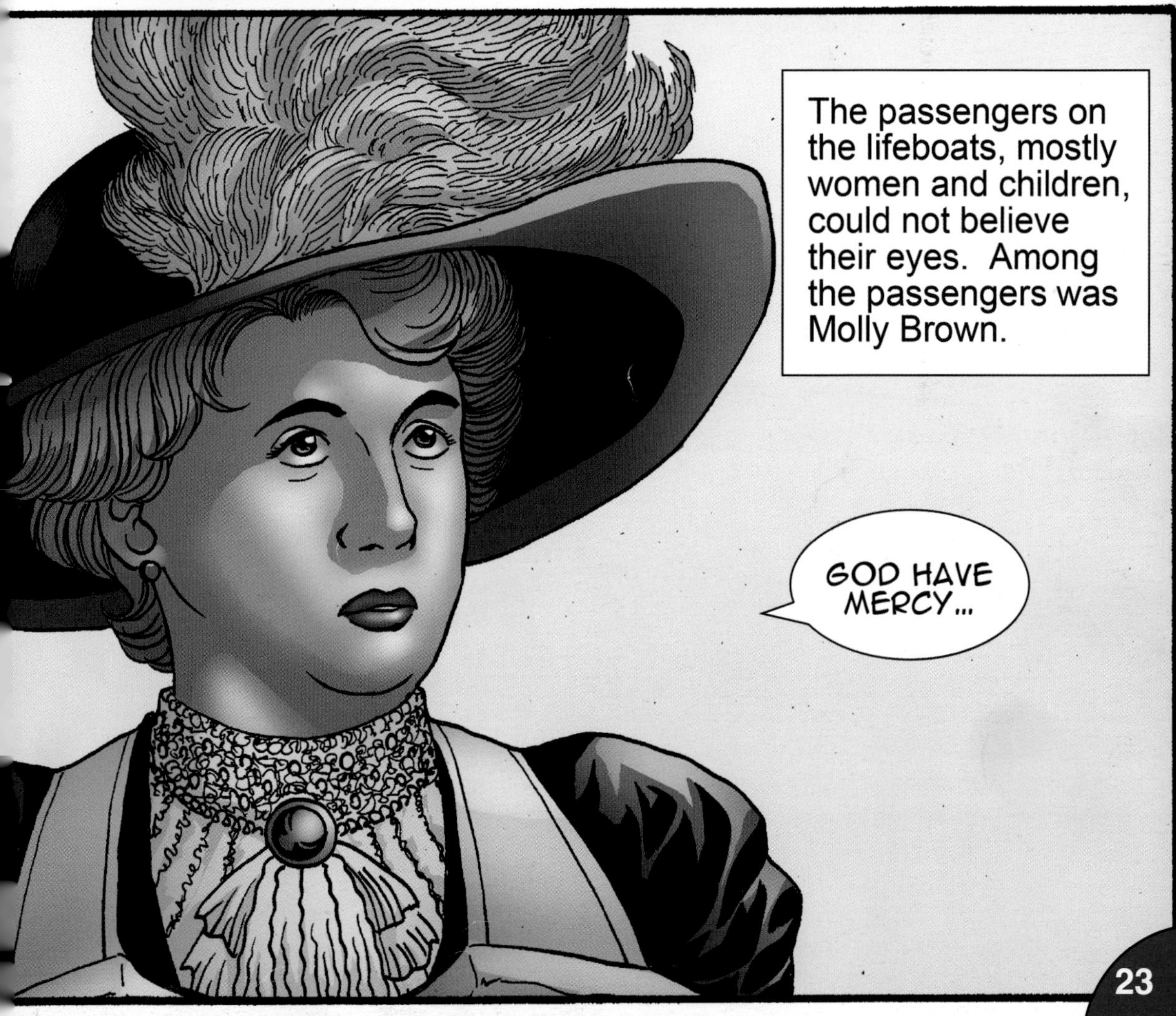
The passengers on the lifeboats, mostly women and children, could not believe their eyes. Among the passengers was Molly Brown.
GOD HAVE MERCY...

Chapter 6 The Sinking of the Unsinkable

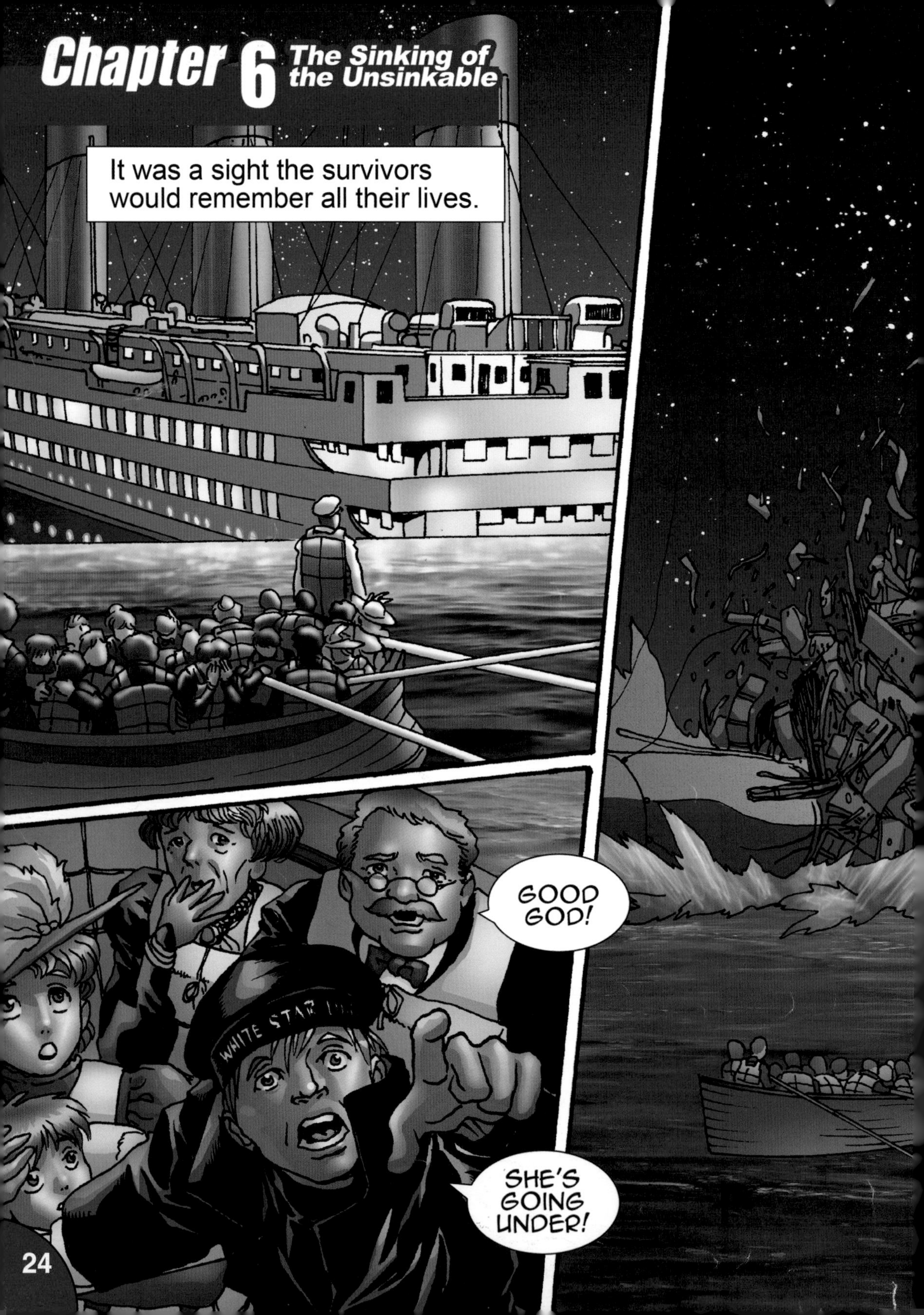
It was a sight the survivors would remember all their lives.
GOOD GOD!
SHE'S GOING UNDER!

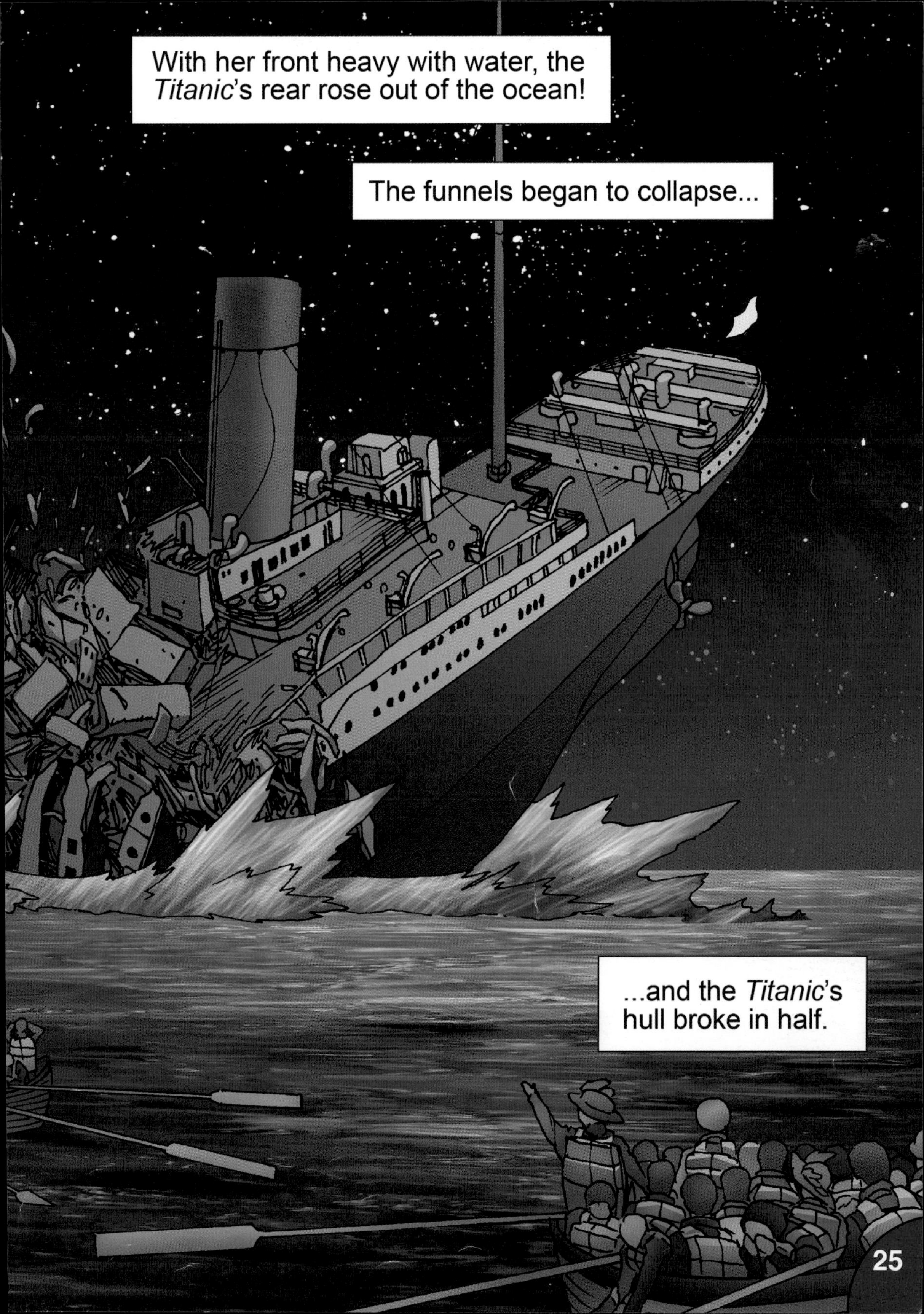
With her front heavy with water, the *Titanic*'s rear rose out of the ocean!
The funnels began to collapse...
...and the *Titanic*'s hull broke in half.

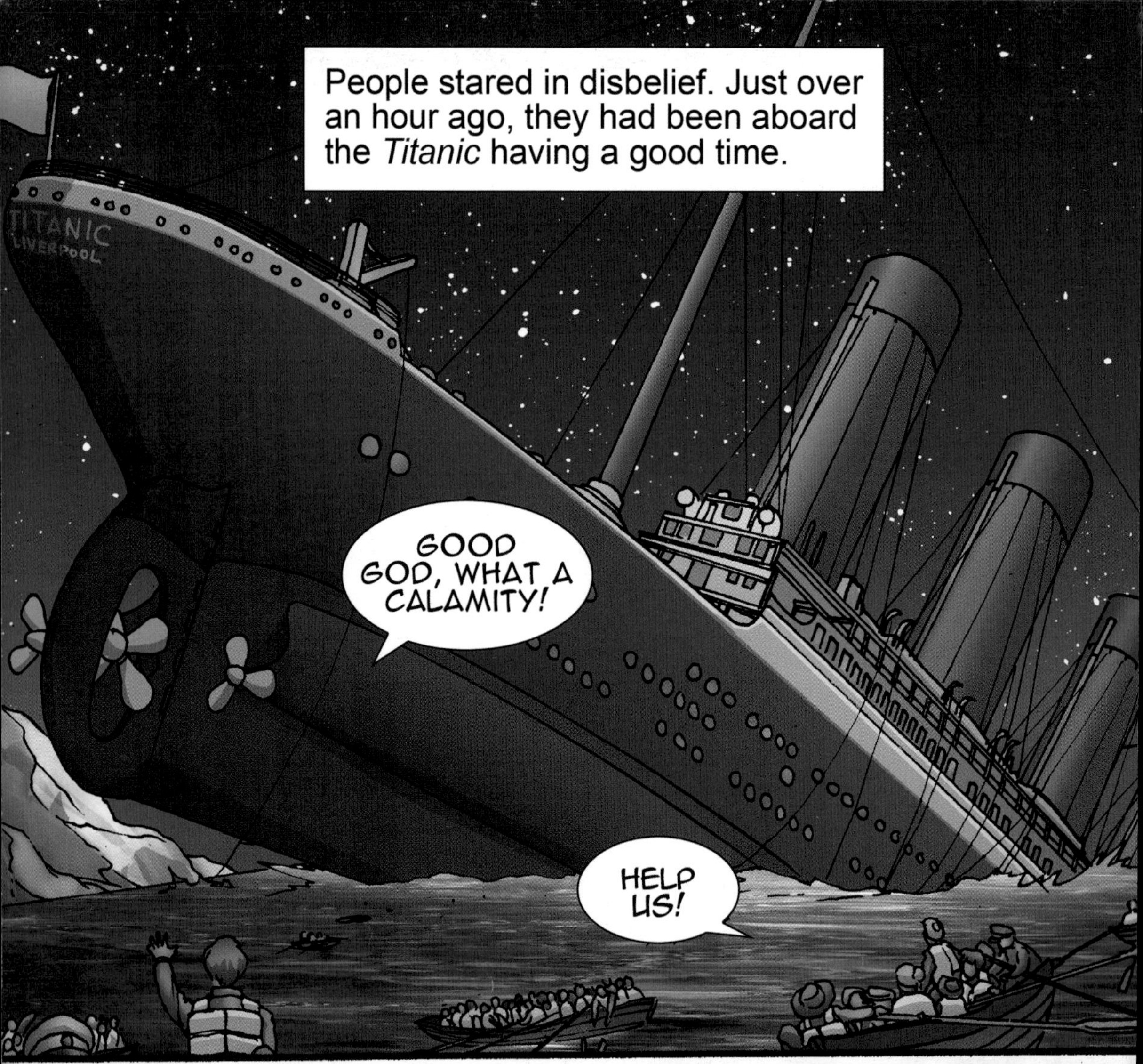
People stared in disbelief. Just over an hour ago, they had been aboard the *Titanic* having a good time.
TITANIC
LIVERPOOL
GOOD GOD, WHAT A CALAMITY!
HELP US!

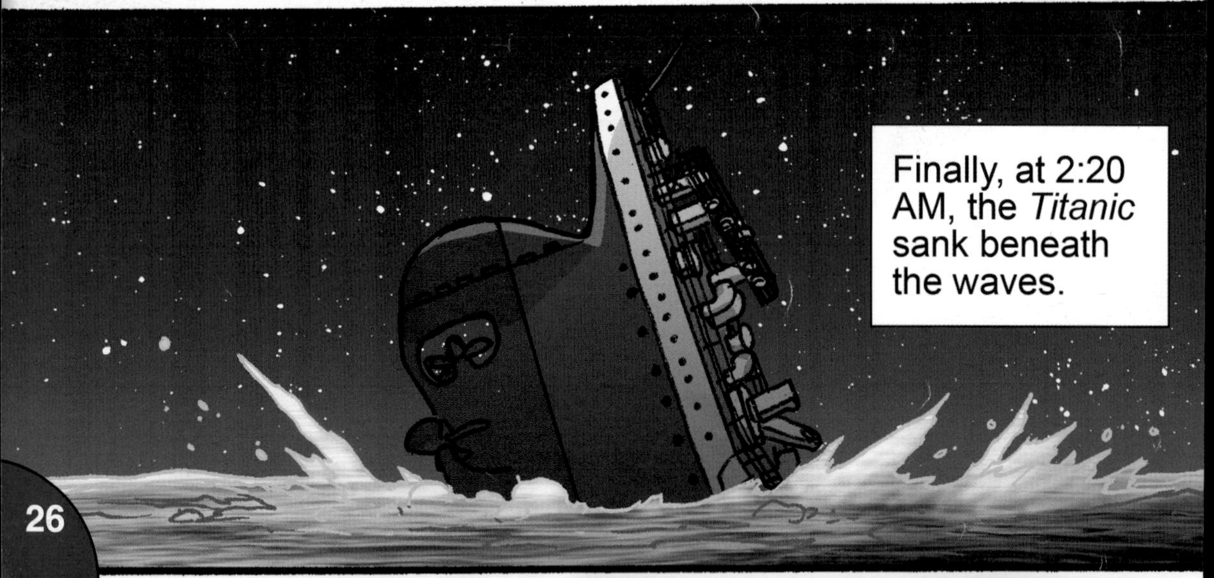
Finally, at 2:20 AM, the *Titanic* sank beneath the waves.

Chapter 7 Rescued at Last

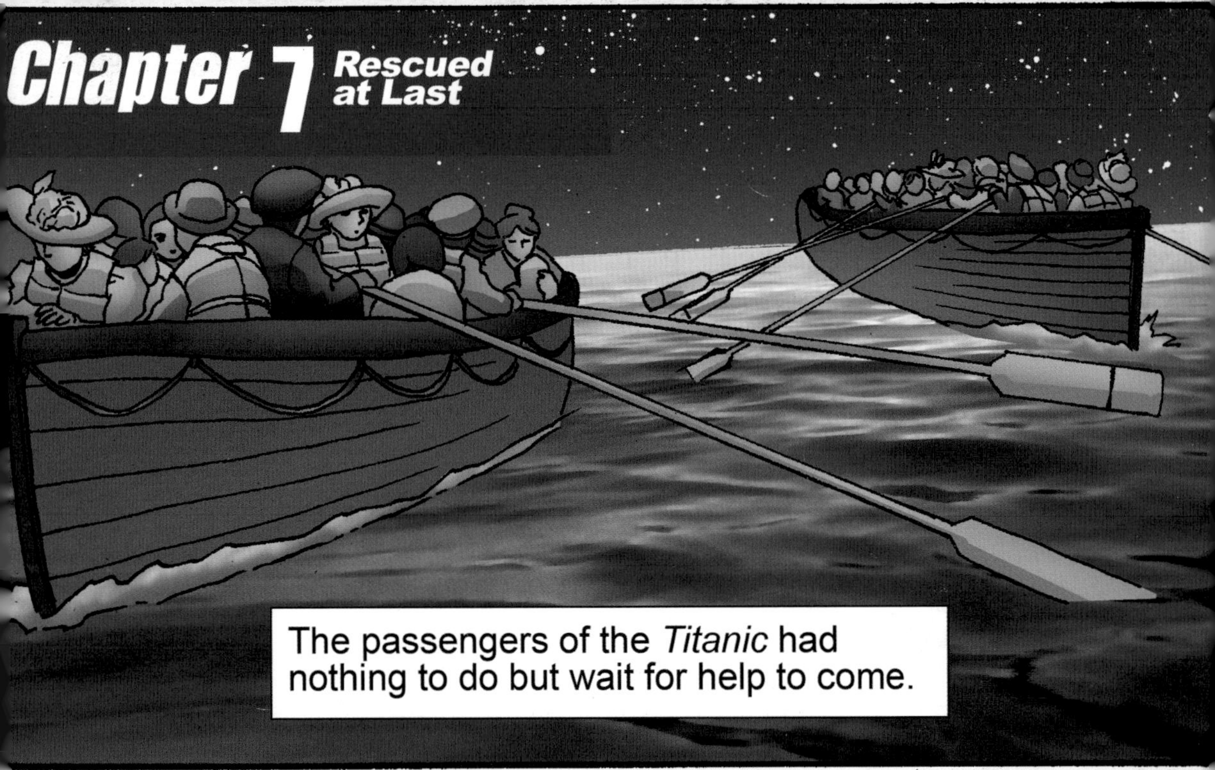

The passengers of the *Titanic* had nothing to do but wait for help to come.

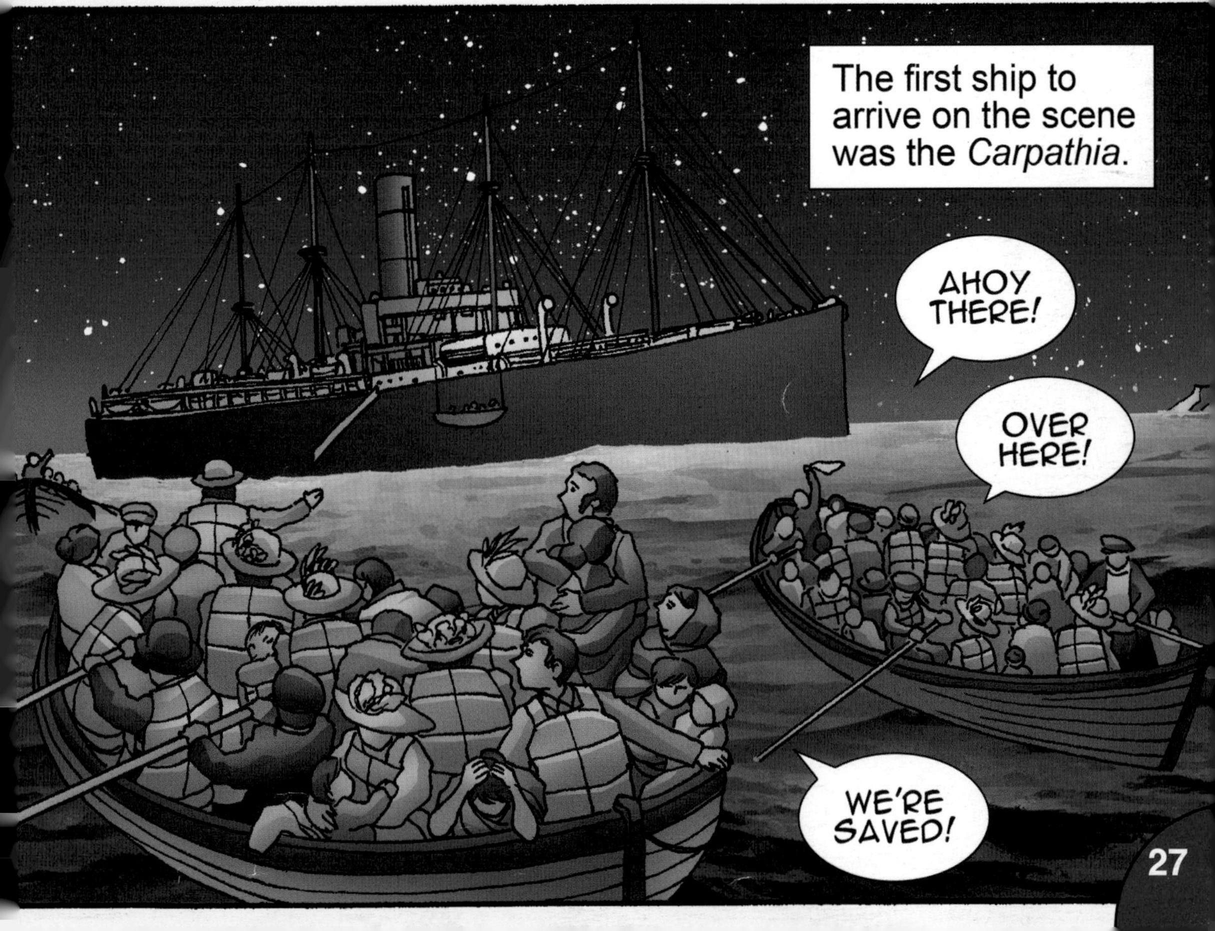

The first ship to arrive on the scene was the *Carpathia*.
AHOY THERE!
OVER HERE!
WE'RE SAVED!

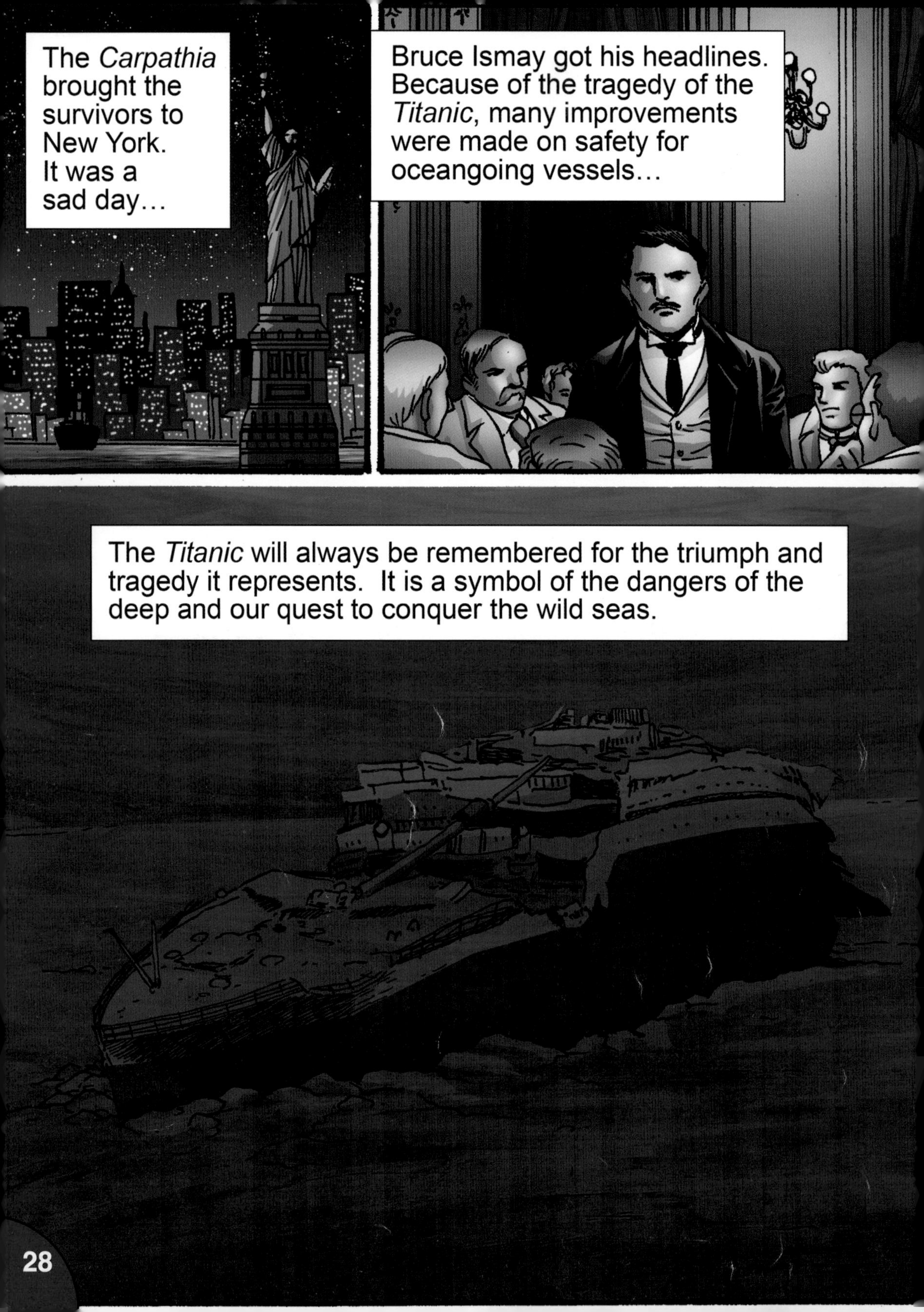
The Carpathia brought the survivors to New York. It was a sad day…
Bruce Ismay got his headlines. Because of the tragedy of the Titanic, many improvements were made on safety for oceangoing vessels…
The Titanic will always be remembered for the triumph and tragedy it represents. It is a symbol of the dangers of the deep and our quest to conquer the wild seas.

Titanic Facts

Titanic's Builder:
Shipbuilding firm of Harland and Wolff

Location Built: **Belfast, Ireland**
Owned By: **Oceanic Steam Navigation Company**
Construction Began: **March 22, 1909**
Construction Completed: **May 31, 1911**
Launched: **April 10, 1912**

Ship's Length: **882 feet, 8 inches**
Ship's Width: **92 feet, 6 inches**
Ship's Weight: **52,310 tons or 117,174 pounds**
Ship's Horsepower: **50,000 hp**
Ship's Passengers: **1,316**
    First class: **325**
    Second class: **285**
    Third class: **706**
Crew: **885**

Iceberg Struck: **April 14, 1912, at 11:40 PM**
Titanic Sank: **April 15, 1912, at 2:20 AM**

Location of Wreck: **963 miles northeast of New York and 453 miles southeast of Newfoundland coastline, 2.5 miles beneath the ocean's surface**

Route of the Titanic

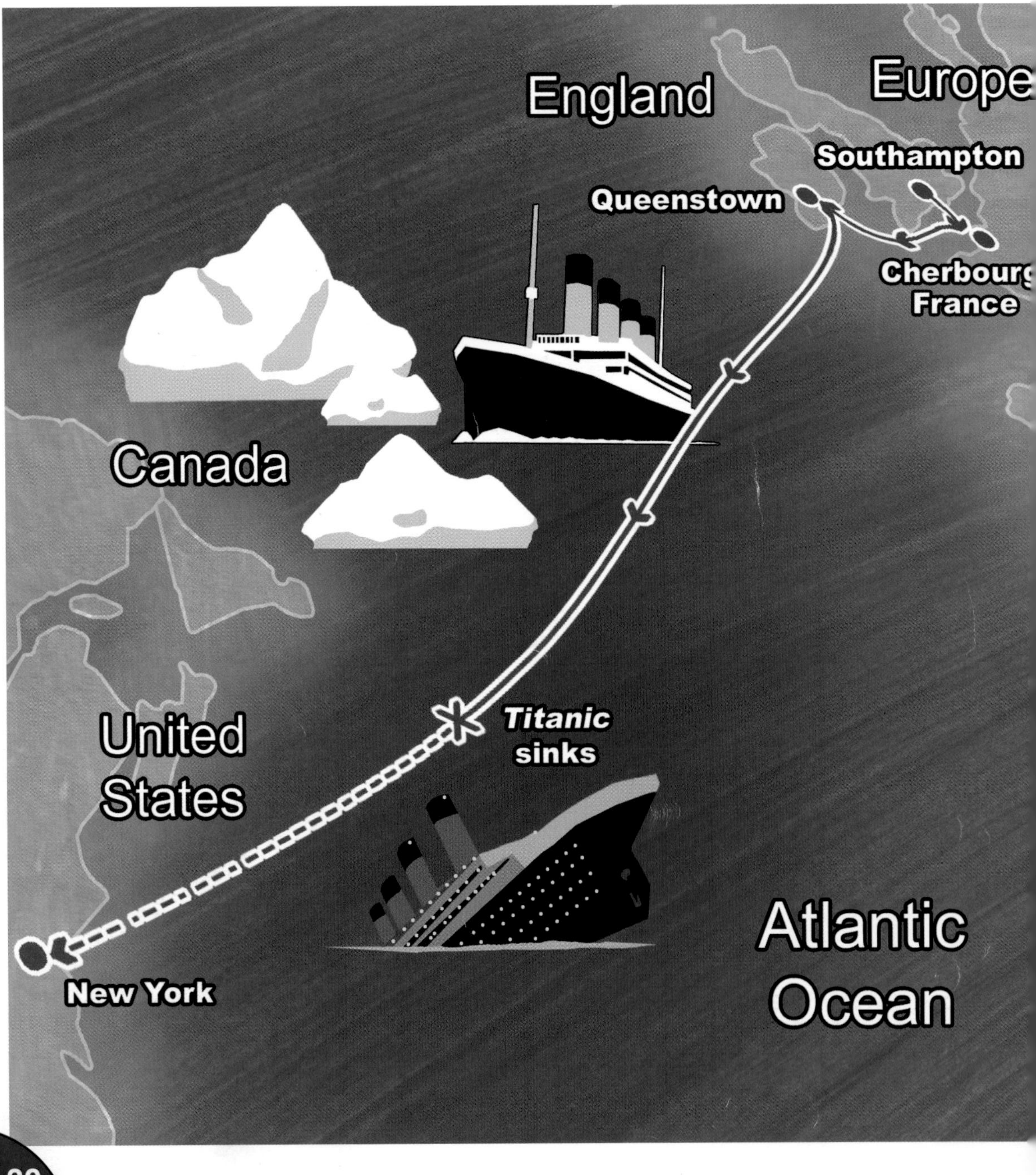
England
Europe
Southampton
Queenstown
Cherbourg
France
Canada
United States
Titanic sinks
Atlantic Ocean
New York

Glossary

calamity - a disastrous event that caused many deaths.

collision - when two items crash into each other.

hull - the frame of a ship.

immigrate - to enter another country to live. A person who immigrates is called an immigrant.

keel - the main part of a ship that develops its structure. A keel runs on the bottom of the ship from front to back along the centerline.

mooring - a chain or line that keeps a thing in one place.

outfit - to equip a ship with items needed for a voyage.

starboard - the right side of a ship or aircraft when facing forward.

Web Sites

To learn more about the *Titanic*, visit ABDO Publishing Company on the World Wide Web at **www.abdopublishing.com.** Web sites about the *Titanic* are featured on our Book Links page. These links are routinely monitored and updated to provide the most current information available.

Index

A

Andrews, Thomas 6, 17, 21
Atlantic Ocean 11, 25

B

boilers 10, 13
Brown, Molly 12, 23

C

Carpathia 27, 28
Cunard Lines 5

E

emergency watertight
  compartments 6, 17, 20
engines 10, 13

F

first-class passengers 8, 19, 22
France 9

H

Harland and Wolff 5
hull 5, 25

I

icebergs 13, 14, 15, 16
Ireland 9
Ismay, Bruce 5, 12, 13, 17, 28

K

keel 5

L

lifeboats 12, 17, 23

M

Murdoch 10

N

New York 9
New York City 7, 11, 13, 28

O

Olympic 5

P

propellers 10

S

second-class passengers 8, 19
Smith, Edward J. 7, 10, 13, 17,
  21
Southampton 7

T

third-class passengers 8, 19, 22
trial runs 5